TERESA RADOMSKA

BASED
RECOLLEC

T0326020

MIDNIGHT
TRAIN ★ TO SIBERIA

**A POLISH FAMILY'S COURAGE IN SURVIVING
THE WARTIME HELL CREATED BY STALIN**

TERESA RADOMSKA

BASED ON THE PERSONAL
RECOLLECTIONS OF ALICJA GORAL

MIDNIGHT
TRAIN ★ TO SIBERIA

**A POLISH FAMILY'S COURAGE IN SURVIVING
THE WARTIME HELL CREATED BY STALIN**

MEREO
Cirencester

Mereo Books

1A The Wool Market Dyer Street Cirencester Gloucestershire GL7 2PR
An imprint of Memoirs Publishing www.mereobooks.com

Midnight train to Siberia: 978-1-909544-76-5

First published in Great Britain in 2014
by Mereo Books, an imprint of Memoirs Publishing

The address for Memoirs Publishing Group Limited can be found at
www.memoirspublishing.com

The Memoirs Publishing Group Ltd Reg. No. 7834348

The Memoirs Publishing Group supports both The Forest Stewardship Council® (FSC®) and
the PEFC® leading international forest-certification organisations. Our books carrying both the
FSC label and the PEFC® and are printed on FSC®-certified paper. FSC® is the only
forest-certification scheme supported by the leading environmental organisations including
Greenpeace. Our paper procurement policy can be found at
www.memoirspublishing.com/environment

Typeset in 11.5/16pt Plantin
by Wiltshire Associates Publisher Services Ltd. Printed and bound in Great Britain by
Printondemand-Worldwide, Peterborough PE2 6XD

CONTENTS

POLAND 1921 – 1939

Alicja's home town,
(now part of Ukraine)

ALICJA'S JOURNEY FROM POLAND TO ENGLAND

My mother Alicja Hartley, née Goral, lived and continues to live the story related in these pages. I hope I have been able to give enough insight into her early life to enable her grandchildren and future generations to understand her and her remarkable family.

In memory of

Kazia   Adam   Walery   Ziuta

Jasia   Janusz   Wlodek   Zbyszek   Marysia

Teresa Radomska 2013

ACKNOWLEDGEMENTS AND SOURCES

I gratefully acknowledge a number of other people's efforts,
and am indebted to the writers of the many books I read whilst
researching this period in Poland's history.

Stolen Childhood – Lucjan Krolikowski

Stalin's Ethnic Cleansing in Eastern Poland – Association of the
Families of the Borderland Settlers

Forgotten Polish Deportees – William Chodkiewicz

The General Langfitt Story

Polish Deportees in The Soviet Union – Michael Hope

The History of Poland, The Second World War – M Kasprzyk

My Life in Exile – Danuta Gradosielska (A Friend of the Family)

God's Playground, A History of Poland – Norman Davies

My thanks to the many members of my extended family who
provided such a wonderful archive of photos and personal recollections.
I also gratefully acknowledge the permission granted by Ryszard Grzybowski
of the Association of the Families of the Eastern Borderlands to use artwork
and poems reproduced in this book.

Alec Dyki

Anita de Haan

Janina Misik

Marek, Ania and Ewa Skoczylas

Kazia and Adam Goral

Alicja Goral Hartley

INTRODUCTION

On 1st September 1939 1.8 million German troops invaded Poland on three fronts, East Prussia in the north, Germany in the west and Slovakia in the south. They had 2600 tanks against the Polish 180, and over 2000 aircraft against the Poles' 420. On 29th September Poland was partitioned according to the Soviet-Nazi 'non aggressive' pact. The two nations each specified their territorial claims, which divided Poland along the Ribbentrop-Molotov Line. Eastern Poland was given to the Soviet Union and the whole of the western and central territories to Germany.

On 17th September Russia invaded from the East on the pretext of helping Poland against the Germans. Instead, one of Stalin's first moves was to deport the military families, priests, lawyers, professors, the society élite of Poland, to Siberia. These included the families of the eastern Borderlands.

On 10th February 1940 the Russians began a deportation programme, sending Poles to Siberian labour camps in four phases up to 1941. In June 1941 Germany attacked Russia, which was no longer her ally. Hitler was getting greedy and when Russia became an ally of Britain, an amnesty was decreed (on Churchill's orders) for all Poles on Russian soil. The subsequent Polish-Russian pact, signed by General Sikorsky and the Soviet Ambassador, Iwan Maisky, in the presence of Churchill and Eden, provided for the creation of a Polish Army and an amnesty for all Polish citizens in Russia, and discharge of the Poles from the labour camps. There was no help from the Russians by way of transport or food; in fact they went out of their way to disrupt the programme.

This is the story of the travels and endurance of one of the families who were deported to Russia: my mother Alicja, her sister Jasia, her brother Janusz and her parents Kazia and Adam, together with Kazia's brother Walery and his family. It tells how they were awakened in the early hours of the bitterly cold Friday of 10th February 1940 by soldiers of the Russian NKVD, the precursor to the KGB, carrying guns, and taken to assembly points in Rowne. From there they were transported in cattle trucks across the deep snows of Russia and Siberia to Sharya, where the rail tracks came to an end, and they had to walk through deep snow to the labour camps of Poldniewica, later to Duraszewo and finally to Derewalka. Their only crime was being Polish.

They were expected to work for their communist masters, clearing forests to lay tracks for a railway from dawn to dusk on meagre rations. Many perished through malnutrition, disease and the cold. A deportee was a 'non-person', a slave of the Soviet penal system. Upon arrival at the prison, labour camp or penal colony they were told by the Commandant: 'Here you will live and here you will die, *niechevo*, hairs will grow on my palms before you are free.'

By the middle of 1940 some one and a half million surviving Polish citizens had been imprisoned in subhuman conditions throughout Russia, from the Caucasus to the White Sea, in steppe, tundra and taiga, from the Urals to the mountains of Russian Asia. At the same time 222,000 Polish servicemen were imprisoned in Siberian Gulags. Once the amnesty was declared in 1941 and they had received discharge papers and been given their freedom, they were faced with yet another journey, this time through Siberia to Uzbekistan and then Persia (modern Iran) and onto the Lebanon in the Middle East. Like many Poles freed from imprisonment in Russia, they were determined to join the Polish Army gathering in Tashkent.

Another struggle for survival began. They had very little food to sustain them, were often ill with dysentery and typhus and my grandmother suffered a severe heart condition. They were separated from each other at times, but with great determination they journeyed on. In Uzbekistan, where they were reunited, my mother, aunt and uncle joined the Polish cadets, while my grandfather joined the Polish army in Iraq. They now had time to rest, recuperate and eventually find work.

My mother somehow found time to fall in love with

and marry an Englishman serving in the RAF, which precipitated yet another journey, from Lebanon to England. My parents disembarked from the *Durban Castle* on 9th November 1945 to begin a new life. For my mother, it was freedom at last. The remainder of the family were reunited in England some time later.

The end of the war had brought about the complete sellout of Poland to Russian oppression, an unexpected blow to the many Poles dispersed throughout the world. The matter of returning home suddenly ceased to be taken for granted. How could one return to a communist Poland, a dictatorship? Unless you were a communist there was no future in Poland.

My mother made another long journey recently, this time through her memories, to put all that happened into a story so that her grandchildren will know just how far she travelled and why. This is her story, with additional material added from research to paint the picture as vividly as possible. It is dedicated to my mother and to the memory of my grandparents and Great Uncle Walery and his family. Their courage in defying immeasurable human suffering is hugely significant and must be acknowledged. Stalin deported at least 1.8 million Poles to Siberia and other bleak outposts of Russia, but not many Western history books record this episode. No politicians honour the victims in speeches commemorating World War II. Yet accounts of the war are incomplete without this neglected historical tragedy.

I am conscious of my roots as a daughter of the eastern Borderland survivors, settlers who were the Red Army's first target on entering Poland. Their aim was to crush these military families in an act of revenge and retaliation, and there was no place for this 'clique' in the Soviet order. Stalin had not forgotten the defeat in the 1920 Polish-Bolshevik war.

I hope my contribution to these memoirs has done justice to the memory of my beloved grandparents, Kazia and Adam and the other members of the family, Walery, Ziuta and family, all linked to the names of Radomski and Goral.

The story continues with the combined thoughts, memories and research of mother and daughter: Alicja Hartley, formerly Goral, and myself.

Teresa Radomska, 2013

CHAPTER ONE

A PEACEFUL CHILDHOOD

This is a story of the deportation of Polish citizens, including my family, by the Russians, and the partitioning of my country into the hands of the Soviet Union and Germany, yet another example of German and Soviet greed for Polish territories.

The Nazi terror unleashed in Europe from 1939 to 1945 was based on a primitive pseudo-scientific theory of race, and was unprecedented in the history of Poland and indeed the world. Our people were essentially in a state of slavery. Between five and six million Polish citizens fell victim to the Nazis, half of them Jews. Stalin's 'Eastern Plan' included a scheme to deport Poles to Siberia and other remote Russian territories, and this was partially accomplished with further loss of life to the Poles of over 2 million.

It began on August 23rd 1939, when the Hitler-Stalin pact was signed. The pact contained a secret protocol concerning the renewed partition of Poland along the Ribbentrop-Molotov Line. The Second World War was sparked off by an attack by the German army on the Polish

munitions depot on the Westerplatte in Gdansk, at dawn on September 1st. Great Britain declared war on Germany two days later.

On September 17th the Polish units, fighting alone, were attacked from the rear by the Red Army, which went on to take control of more than half of Poland. On September 27th, after a siege lasting almost three weeks, Warsaw surrendered to the Germans, and by October 5th all resistance by the Polish Army had ceased.

Map showing the partition of Poland according to the Soviet-Nazi agreement of September 28, 1939. The territory of the Polish Republic in its pre-World War II boundaries was divided along the so-called Ribbentrop-Molotov Line.

I was born on 19th February 1924 in Lipniki, a small village in Eastern Poland which after the Yalta Conference in 1945 was to come under Russian rule and become part of Russia's growing empire. It was soon after the First World War and times were very hard; Poland was still recovering from that conflict and my parents had had a very difficult time. They had met after my father, Adam Goral, had joined the Cavalry (*Krechowieka*) in 1914 to fight for his beloved country to free Poland from oppression. He was only 17 when he enlisted.

Adam's mother, my grandmother Konstancja, had met and fallen in love with a Polish count, Erazma Rupniewski. They had an affair, but Rupniewski did not love her and refused to support his son (a story appeared in the *Polish Gazette* in 1997 about a Castellan Rupniewski going back to the 18th century who had a castle in Sytdow). My father became very bitter about these circumstances and how harshly his mother had been treated and could never come to terms with the fact that he was illegitimate. All his life he carried his remorse over the fact that in a moment of weakness his mother had allowed herself to be seduced by this nobleman who had refused to play his rightful role and be father to his illegitimate child, support him and give him an education. The stigma of illegitimacy was something to be greatly ashamed of in those days and he never forgave his mother or Rupniewski for their actions. He was never able to meet Rupniewski to make his feelings known and the plight of the Rupniewski family is not known.

*Alicja in Lipniki around
1926 with cousin Leon*

Alicja, 2005

Wladyslaw, around 1917

Adam, 1917

Konstancia later married Boleslaw Goral, who brought up
my father, and eventually he acquired a half-brother and
sisters, Boleslaw, Steffa and Bronia. My grandmother lived
to be 105, an incredible age. My father's participation in

the Great War had left a tremendous impact on his psyche; he was at times very quiet and seemed lost in his thoughts. When he was older he moved from central Poland to the eastern side, which was not so wealthy and needed help with the rebuilding of its land and the economy. My mother Kazia (Kazimiera) lived at that time on an estate called Rozienek, where her father, Wladislaw Radomski, also from the Polish nobility, was the estate manager. He was the son of Wladyslaw, a nobleman whose coat of arms in official papers of that time identified his true name as Bielawski; his estate had been lost in the uprising, in which he had participated in 1863 against the Russians.

From the 17th century, Poland had been occupied by the three great powers of the time, Austria, Prussia (the leading state of the country we know now as Germany) and Russia. As punishment for his involvement in that uprising, Wladislaw was sentenced to serve time in a prison camp in Siberia, but through incredible good luck and his few useful connections among the elite he was able to escape from the prison where he was being held in Poland. He then changed his name from Bielawski to Radomski. He was able to find work on the estate of Count Szczerbek as an administrator. My mother Kazia was therefore brought up by him and her mother Sophia and siblings in a manor house. Her brothers and sisters were Antony, Bronia, Walery, Tolus and Gienia. When her father died the family moved to eastern Poland, where they lived in relative poverty in comparison to what they had been used to.

It was on that large estate, where my grandfather was

the manager, that Adam met and fell in love with Kazia, my mother, the beautiful Kazimiera. After proposing to Kazia and being accepted, Adam went off to war. He had promised her, with the bravado of a young cavalryman, that the enemy bullets would not get him and he would return, and true to his word he came back from the war and married my mother in 1923.

Soon after, my father was granted some land by the government in return for his war service and my parents settled on Osada (settlement) Krechowiecka near Wolyn, not far from the Ukrainian/Russian border, where other settlers had also built their homes. His regiment had been the 1st Lancers Krechowiecki.

Kazia and Adam, 1920

Kazia Radomska, 1920

Adam Goral, 1917   *Ziuta and Kazia*

My father built a bungalow there and my parents and their growing family were settled there happily for some years. Many Polish soldiers and their families were granted small plots of land as a reward for their patriotism and to help re-establish Polish claims to the area. My father had fought in the 1914-18 war and in the Polish-Russian uprising in 1920 and had earned the right to the land.

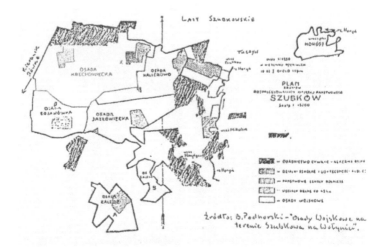

Osada Krechowiecka – settled by the families Goral and Radomski

Wolyn, Powiat Rowne, Gmina Aleksandria was settled in the spring of 1921 by soldiers of the 1st Pulk Ulanow Krechowieckich (Lancers).

LIST OF SETTLERS AT OSADA KRECHOWIECKA
(partial list)

mjr Edward Milewski
Jakub Chromik
Feliks Bojankiewicz
Wachm. Adam Goral
Wadyslaw Gorzkowski
plut. Gustaw Chanecki
kpr. Franciszek Gorczak
st. ul. Franciszek Galka
plut. Jozef Brzostowski

ul. Franciszek Sterna
ul. Stanislaw Graniczny
wachm. Jan Szymanski
por. Edward Czajkowski
wachm. Piotr Swojnog
ul. Walery Radomski
st. wachm. Stanislaw Armatys
st. ul. Antoni Kulik
ul. Stanislaw Wojna
ul. Karol Kalusiewicz Wladyslaw Szymanik
ul. Wojciech Morozowicz
ul. Stefan Prochera
Jozef Zwolinski
Rormuald Graniczny
Jozef Ogonowski
Wojciech Zygadlo
Jozef Wrzyszcz
Adolf Zajdel
Jozef Szopa
ul. Bronislaw Kucharewicz
Zygmunt Walasiewicz
Jan Zdanek
ul. Modest Los
ul. Wladyslaw Paszynski
Jan Madej
Bernard Bujnowski
Kazimierz Kaczmarski
Jan Jankowski
Stefan Swierczynski
st. wachm.
Jozef Manka Stefan Dobrzanski
st. wachm. Klemens Grzybowski
Wincenty Rzonca
Stanislaw Boryn
plut. Stanislaw Pukacz

Adam and Walery, 1918

Walery, 1918

Osada Krechowiecka, north east of Rowne, 1930s

The Osada Krechowiecka is now called Nova Ukrainka and belongs to the Ukrainian republic. All towns and villages have been renamed since the Yalta Convention in 1945. My sister was born in a village named Swiatje, west of Aleksandria, now renamed Svyattya, and Rowne is now called Rivne.

Nova Ukrainka

Jobs were very hard to find and the land wasn't paying enough to keep the family, so my father decided to go further afield and got a job in Rowne. Soon the family, including by this time three children, myself (born 1924), Jasia, my younger sister (born 1926) and Janusz, the youngest, born in 1930, moved with him. In Rowne life was good. We lived in a big apartment by the river and we children went to a school named after our Queen, Jadwiga. We were happy, but there was always a worry about my mother, who had a heart complaint and suffered very frequent attacks, which caused anxiety to the family.

On summer vacation we used to return to our estate, the Osada Krechowiecka, or to my Uncle Walery's Osada a little further away. We had wonderful times with Uncle Walery. We slept in the barn in the hay, and I remember one night there was a terrible storm which lasted all night and scared us all. We didn't stay in the barn for long. We ran in the pouring rain across to the bungalow, knocking on the door and waking my aunt and uncle to let us in. It had been an exciting adventure, but a very short one!

Patrol of the 1st Krechowiecki Lancers, c 1919

Tolus, Bronia, Kazia, Walery, friend, 1920

Tolus, 1917

Genia, 1928

Ziuta, Walery's wife, 1919

Walery, 1919

Kazia, 1920

Adam, 1920

Sophia Radomska, 1930   *Wladislaw Bielawski-Radomski, 1920*

Beilawski-Radomski Family, 1930

Radomski brothers and sisters

Tolus, 1917

Kazia, 1937

Walery, 1920

Gienia, 1937

We became friendly with a family in the apartment where we lived, with three boys and a girl. One of the boys, Rysiek, was 16, and had a crush on me. Two older men were also showing an interest in me, but as I was only 16 I just brushed them aside, wondering why they were interested in such a young girl. I was growing up and my father seemed concerned. We lived quietly and comfortably, getting on with our lives day to day. We were aware of some unrest, but totally unprepared for the horrors soon to be unleashed upon us.

Jasia, Halina, Janusz,
Ala, Rowne, 1934

Ala, Halina, Jasia,
Janusz, Rowne, 1934

Walery's Osada, Kazia, Adam, Ziuta, 1937

The church in Rowne

Ala, 1938

The Goral family on the way to church in Rowne, 1936

Alicja, 1938

Janusz and Adam, Rowne, 1936　　*Kazia, Adam, Janusz, Rowne, 1939*

Janusz, Ala, Kazia, Jasia, Rowne, 1937

POLAND'S TROUBLED HISTORY

I want to illustrate how hard Poland has had to fight for its very existence – especially against Russia. Our written history begins in the 10th century, when Poland was ruled by a dynasty called the Piasts. Mieszko Piast I reigned from about 960-999. In 966 he became a Christian and his people followed his example. Poland's history from then on is a troubled one, of many struggles, facing threat after threat to her borders from as early as 1241 and through to 1916 from the Mongols, the Teutonic Knights, Ukrainians, Swedes, Turks, the French, Prussians, Austrians, Germans and Russians, all helping themselves to Polish territory, which was beautiful with plentiful natural resources.

Poland has seen ages of economic prosperity and peace, military success and revivals of learning, but more often than not she has been defeated and weakened by enemies who joined forces with others against her. This story demonstrates the absolute antipathy between Poland and Russia. Poland seems to have been portrayed by

Russia as an anarchic, dangerous country, its Catholic faith and democratic ideas requiring suppression by its more 'enlightened' neighbour.

The two countries have long histories, dating to the late Middle Ages, and relations have always been tense. The Kingdom of Poland and the Grand Duchy of Muscovy have struggled for control of their borderlands and over the centuries there have been several Polish-Russian wars, the catalyst being the Polish union with Lithuania (1386), which brought Catholic Poland and Orthodox Russia into a continuing state of unrest. There have been other wars, with many other enemies intent on conquering and dividing up Poland, but Russia has been the foremost aggressor, her only ambition having been to keep Poland weak and divided, suppressing Polish culture and imposing her will. This has proved extremely difficult, as Polish culture and political activity have continued to flourish. The Poles have never been suppressed for long, however hard her enemies tried to impose their will. The Poles' strength of human spirit and Catholic faith was unbreakable and will have seen them through each conflict.

For example, in 1794 the Poles were crushed by the Prussians and Russians, who together with Austria in 1795 went on to divide the last part of Poland between them. The Polish King Stanislaw August abdicated and the Polish Commonwealth (Rzeczpospolita) ceased to exist, removed from the map of Europe in stages known as 'the partitions' of which there were three. It was deprived of its sovereignty for 123 years. Today Poland is a member of NATO and of the EU.

Poland regained her freedom in 1918 after being proclaimed an independent country, though she faced yet more unrest and uprisings from neighbouring countries, the Bolshevik Ukraine, Germany, Lithuania and Czechoslovakia. There was another longer war between the two main protagonists from 1919-1921, and in 1920 the Polish army, against massive odds, stopped the advance of the Bolshevik army and gained big territories in the east.

A more recent war has been fought against the Russians for freedom, from the communist tyranny imposed post-WW2, a fight between the workers and the Jaruzelski government, which imposed martial law. The Solidarity movement ended this in 1988/89 when the communists gave in and elections were eventually held. In 1991 the Warsaw Pact (signed in 1955 to compete with NATO, comprising USSR, Eastern Germany, Poland, Czechoslavkia, Hungary, Bulgaria and Romania) was dissolved and the Cold War was officially over. Since the fall of communism in both Poland and Russia relations have entered a new phase, seeing both improvement and deterioration as measured by various factors.

It is difficult to foresee what the future holds for Poland, but it is to be hoped that European Union membership will be beneficial. Poland seems to be safer from Russian colonialism now than at any time in its history. However, there are constant issues, one being that Poland is moving towards the West and away from the Russian sphere of influence (joining NATO and the EU) and pursuing an independent political stance. Relations worsen at remembrance of historical events, like the Katyn massacre, which Poland sees as genocide and Russia as a war crime. Poland supported the democratic Orange revolution in the Ukraine (2004). Russians in turn criticised Poland's perceived lack of gratitude for liberation from Nazi occupation, ignoring their own occupation of Poland, the many deportations and atrocities.

In 2008 there was a dramatic worsening of relations in the South Ossetia war, Poland taking a leading role in the intervention of the international community on the side of Georgia against Russia. An agreement between Poland and the US allowing the US to install an interceptor defence shield earned the response from Russia that it made Poland "a legitimate military target". Russia later announced that it was to set up missiles in Kaliningrad, close to Poland. Exercise Zapad in September 2009 involved a simulated nuclear attack against Poland, the suppression of an uprising by a Polish minority in Belarus and many other operations of an aggressive nature. They continue to the present day.

The recent election results in Russia (March 2012), which gave Vladimir Putin enormous majorities for a landslide election to the presidency and his party to the Duma (council assemblies, governmental institutions created by Tsar Nicholas II) exposed corruption on a massive scale. Independent monitors declared the election 'hugely unfair and skewed in Putin's favour'.

The result, although expected - the ceremonial dais

was out well before the result - resulted in tens of thousands of very brave and very angry young demonstrators gathering in Moscow's Pushkin Square defying the vast police and army clampdown across Moscow, chanting 'Russia without Putin'. There were ugly clashes and many activists were detained at Lubyanka Square, which is in the shadow of the FSB headquarters, site of the notorious prison, and countless ordinary demonstrators were arrested. There were also many arrests in St Petersburg.

Putin was openly mocked when he claimed the poll was 'open and honest' but as the opposition leader, Sergei Udaltsov, pointed out, if it had been a free election, why had the streets been flooded with troops? He claimed there were 12,000 police and army personnel who had formed a 'wall of steel' armed with truncheons and dogs.

People had experienced democracy and a good standard of living and freedom under Gorbachev's early leadership, Yeltsin's and then post communism, and did not want to see a return to the hard line of Putin, ex KGB, an advocate of subversion, destabilisation and disinformation, the tried and tested Russian methods of domination.

Mikhael Gorbachev had demanded that Mr Putin withdraw from the presidential elections and that local elections already declared should be cancelled and re-held. It was to no avail. Putin 'won' 64% of the vote and the independent monitors issued a blistering condemnation of the 'serious problems in the unfair election', having found evidence of widespread vote rigging, voters bussed to voting stations to vote several times, and votes fed into voting machines many times!.

Opposition leaders who were barred from contesting the presidential election sought to spark their own 'Arab spring' in charged speeches to over 20,000 people gathered in a very icy Moscow. The word 'revolution' had been voiced. 'If we don't want revolution then we want free elections' said Mikhail Kasyanov, Putin's former premier. 'Otherwise revolution is inevitable.' It will be interesting to watch how future political events unfold, especially for the Poles, who also wish to see a Russia without Putin and the Russians with full democracy.

Russia continues to seek suppression of others, as well as its own people, albeit by a more sophisticated means, the rigged ballot box and offensive military operations on the borders of Poland and the Baltic states among them. Only the higher tiers of Russia's new democracy are equal, living in opulence. Everybody else is just as the Poles were considered to be, 'non persons'.

INVASION

Life as we knew it ended with Hitler's attack on Poland and the outbreak of World War II. Our lives were changed dramatically, and for ever.

On 1st September 1939 Hitler attacked my country from the west; I think it was a Friday afternoon. All of a sudden the bombs were falling, causing confusion and chaos. We all ran from the apartment into the courtyard and everywhere the bombs were falling. We were terrified, and our two cats, poor things, were running from room to room, so frightened and confused.

Hitler invades Poland – 1939

Warsaw, 1939

We ran from the apartment in the hope of getting to our osada in the country, where we thought it would be safer. We were hiding in the garden of some friends on the outskirts of town when my Uncle Walery came to rescue us. He had left his osada as soon as he'd heard the bombs with his coach and horses to take us away from Rowne and into the safety of the countryside. We just went with him hurriedly in the clothes we were wearing and covered the 16 kilometres back to the Osada very quickly. I don't know what happened to our cats; we never saw them again.

After a few days, when the bombing had stopped, my father and I went back to the apartment in Rowne to see what was happening. We arrived to find some people who had fled the troubles in Warsaw living there. They had made themselves at home after finding the apartment doors and windows open. We had left in such a panic we hadn't had time to think of security. My father let them stay, but they eventually moved out.

That September was glorious. Nature carried on around us, its pattern unbroken. In the orchards the fruit was ripening and there were sunflowers, my father's favourite flower (which he was later to grow in England). We were approaching the potato season. Our lives and our country meanwhile were being destroyed, and we could do nothing about it. Day by day our country was dying around us.

We heard that some of our relatives who lived in western Poland, in Lodz, were under German occupation. Their husbands had been arrested and two of my father's brothers-in-law were killed when the prison they had been put into was set alight. Other relatives somehow managed to survive the war.

On 17th September the Soviet army entered my country through the eastern borderlands under the false pretence of helping Poland in her fight against Germany. We could see the passing tanks of our 'liberators'. The Russians used their power very quickly to arrest all policemen and Poles of any social standing. Towards the end of September the trains were full of Polish soldiers and officers directed by the Russians deep into the USSR.

This was one of the first targets of the Red Army's attack in 1939, a premeditated act of revenge long in the planning and retaliation for the Battle of the Bolsheviks in 1920. All the military and their families were to be banished from their homes and sent to labour camps, as these military settlers were a particular irritant to Stalin. They were intelligent and hardworking men with minds of their own who would stand up to Stalin's doctrine. They despised communism.

Political groups were organised, made up mostly of Ukrainians. The NKVD (later renamed the KGB) was ostensibly protecting the military settlers, but in fact they were acting as administrators for their occupier-masters, to oversee the Polish inhabitants. Among their first actions was the ousting of military settlers from their properties. They would deceive us by telling us our properties would be safe under the protection of the Soviet authorities, but they were already dividing settlers' belongings such as livestock and farm machinery amongst themselves. However, there were also a few good souls amongst them who did help us. Some families refused outright to be moved. Those who had been born in the region were allowed to stay, although they had to rescind ownership of their lands to the Russians and take in many Ukrainian and Russian families to lodge with them and 'help' them on their farms.

One evening we were sitting talking at the supper table at my uncle's osada, with only candles for light because we had been told by the Russians to keep all lights down. We were angry and very worried that they had come into our country like thieves, grabbing our land and its people on the pretext of helping us. They had come in the dark with their rifles at the ready, to shoot us if we came out of our homes. That's how they were helping us! We felt completely abandoned by our allies - where were they? There was nothing we could do against our old enemy. Our country was powerless. We had never felt so vulnerable.

Our fears were intensified even further when soon after the Russians invaded Wolyn. We were under occupation by two enemies, and a very different life beckoned. Two dictators were using our homeland for their own ends.

We returned to our now empty apartment and to a very different life. Russian soldiers and tanks were everywhere and our schools were closed to our normal curriculum; only Russian teaching was allowed. They were days of sheer horror, spent avoiding the NKVD militia as best we could. There was very little in the shops, no sugar, salt, soap, and there were long queues for everything. Life was hard, very sad and gloomy, and we felt helpless. Most men had to hide for fear of being arrested and taken away from their families.

My father was one of them, being a military settler who had been in the Cavalry during the First World War and in the Uprising against the Bolsheviks in 1920, he was considered an 'enemy of the state' to the Russians and could have been taken away at any time. Somehow he managed to stay safe by hiding in different places, mostly with friends. The Russians searched our apartment every day for my father and any weapons they thought we might be hiding - it was terrifying. Policemen, prison officers, teachers, doctors, ex-servicemen and members of other services were arrested and taken away and sent to Siberia. It was only a matter of time before it was our turn, and we waited in fear. My mother did her best to ease our concerns, but it didn't really work. We were well aware of what was happening.

On 10th February 1940, a day that will be engraved in my memory for ever, in very heavy snow, at five o'clock in the morning, we were awakened by Russians hammering at the door of our osada and breaking in. We had no idea what was happening and knew it would be useless to ask. Four NKVD militia men told us to get dressed quickly, pack some of our belongings and get outside. We were very frightened. We did not know what was to happen or where they were going to take us. They had guns and were very intimidating.

There was one good Samaritan among the four soldiers, who told us to go down to the cellar and get a sack of potatoes and salt pork from the barrel, staples of every household. My mother knew immediately where we were going; Siberia. My great-grandfather had been sent there after the uprising of 1863.

We were very frightened. Kazia made sure we had things to do, hurrying from one end of the house to the other to focus our minds and not panic. We were so young and so scared. We quickly packed everything we could into a big basket, including our warm clothes. There was a large horse-drawn sledge waiting outside and we realised we could take more than we thought, as well as the potatoes and pork. My mother then dashed back into the house to grab whatever else she could; she even had the presence of mind to take the family photograph albums. I wonder if she knew we'd never come home?

Those photo albums travelled with us over 10,000 miles. They were never mislaid or forgotten about; they went everywhere. This left us a most important record of the family Radomski/Goral.

This poem describes the similar experience of another family who were sent to Siberia at the same time, February 10th 1940.

> *In February's snow-filled sleep our world collapsed,*
> *Its successor perilous – new-shaped existence.*
> *The night-clad Soviet fist directly lunged,*
> *Crushing our nest – the family home.*
> *Coercive hands – calculated, merciless –*

Hammer the door, wrench the handle.
Understanding dawns... here's Nemesis... Nemesis.
A fleeting prayer, 'Lord, by Thy Shielding...'
Carted like cattle, in wagons clamped,
Through merest window's slit beyond our view
Slides our dearest Polish land: sanctum sanctorum,
Europe's usual martyr shedding farewell tears.
What follows – the grey dolour of Russian fields;
Drained, strained comrades on station platforms ranged;
Leaded skies – cloud sheeted;
Listless eyes; life – lost hands;
Vacant steppes, Siberia, the buran's
Disembodied wail;
Kirghiz' indifference.
In gaping Saman shacks the first year groans
Long as eternity – mine-shaft black –
Amid Life's blood-drained emptiness ...
But God stood with us!

Maria Waridoda

We were ordered out and onto the sledge. There were convoys of sledges loaded with families who, like us, had been arrested. It was bitterly cold, probably 30 degrees of frost. We noticed neighbours standing outside their houses watching us go by. Those who had chosen to stay had to relinquish their properties and belongings to the Ukrainians.

We were taken to an assembly point near to the main square where many hundreds of people were gathered.

The NKVD separated the single men from the women and children. They checked the necessary papers and then we waited for further orders and to see what was to happen next. Eventually we were driven on sledges to the outskirts of Rowne, where a very long cattle train was waiting for all of us. There were hundreds of people standing in heavy snow, wrapped up against the cold. Some we knew, many we didn't. There was the family Mitoszewski amongst them from our own apartment block, and thankfully we were together as a family because married men were allowed to be with their families. It would appear that my father, having escaped all the searches made by the Russians, was able to travel with us. Word of the deportations had got through to where he was hiding and he had rushed to the square but had missed us. He then had run like the devil to where the train was waiting and found us.

We were ordered, at gunpoint, by the aggressive, strutting, newly-enlisted Ukrainian militia and armed NKVD, four of them, to get into the wagon. One of the men was a Jew, the local shopkeeper we knew so well. He wouldn't acknowledge us, so we did the same, just in case we made things worse for him and us. The wagon was dark without windows, but with small metal grilles set high in the walls. The good Samaritan who had arrested us was there to help us again. He made sure that our potatoes and barrel of pork and bundles of clothing stayed with us rather than being taken and put into the goods wagon, where we might never have seen it again. The militia confiscated as much as they could; they were ruthless. Any opportunity to settle old wounds (historic animosity never forgotten) they took with sadistic pleasure. But this particular man felt sorry for us - he was only, after all, following orders. I wish I could remember his name. He said to my mother 'you have a lovely daughter', meaning me, but I think he would have helped us regardless, for he had a good heart.

After he'd put us onto the train with what little goods we had, we never saw him again. He had done his job, but with compassion; had the NKVD seen him acting kindly to us he would almost certainly have ended up in Siberia himself, possibly on the same wagon!

Subordination was very quickly dealt with. There was no conversation, no excuses accepted. A bullet was usually a merciful way out.

On that freezing February day, we were locked into our cattle wagon, which was crammed with so many of us sitting on top of cases and bags and mattresses. It was dark and we waited for many hours, the train shunting back and forth.

Then all of a sudden the train slowly moved off. We were bewildered and terrified. Neither children nor adults realised that something even more awful was going to happen. We looked around us, huddled together and waited as a fear came over us that I'll never forget.

Ziuta, with her children Wladek and Marysia, were in another wagon further down the track, but we didn't know this until much late. Her other son, Zbyszek, was with his father Walery. Walery was taking his sister Genia and her daughter Halina to join her husband Wladislaw in western Poland and hopefully to safety. Zbyszek was determined to join the Polish resistance. He was only a boy but he was anxious to do everything he could for Poland. He avoided the deprivations of the Russian labour camps, but what he actually went through must have been equally dreadful. We regrettably do not have many details of his time during this period as he was killed in very controversial circumstances before being able to join his family in England.

JOURNEY INTO HELL

That dreadful journey on that freezing day was part of the first wave of mass deportations of the civilian population, when nearly 250,000 men, women and children were transported to Northern Russian and Siberia. We were carried on a total of 110 cattle trains, each carrying just over 2000 people to various inhospitable destinations in northern Russian, Uzbekistan and other former Russian republics. A second transportation of 330,000, mostly women and children, started on 13th April, when a total of 160 trains dispersed the victims into areas of Asiatic Russia, mainly Kazakhstan and further eastwards to the Altai Kraj. A third deportation was carried out over June 28th and 29th 1940, in which 250,000 victims, mainly Poles from central and western Poland, followed into forced exile. They were moved to the north of Russia around Archangelsk, Sverdlovsk and Novosibirsk and to the Republics of Bashkirska, Maryjska and to the Krasnoyarski Kraj. A fourth wave of deportees totalling 200,000, of which just over half were from the Wilno area, were scattered across various parts of Russia.

When the trains stopped to refuel and were ready to continue the journey, they didn't wait for those who had got off to find food or water or just to stretch their legs. They were left to find their own way to their families. Some never saw each other again.

The deportations continued until June 1941 and by that time approximately 1,680,000 people had been deported. This does not include the prisoners of war deported to the penal Gulags. Officers, professionals and priests were arrested in the winter of 1939 and executed in cold blood. Thousands were found with hands tied behind their backs and a bullet in the base of the skull. It has recently been discovered that the Ukrainian Galiizen Division was probably responsible for massacring Polish citizens during the war. However, the investigations have not so far been able to place the blame categorically where it should lie, though the reasons are as yet not clear. Political agendas may stand in the way of the truth.

Officers were buried in mass graves in the Katyn forest, where 4421 bodies have been found. A total of 250,000 Polish servicemen were separated and placed in three camps, Kozielsk, Starobelsk and Ostashkov. More bodies were found in Starobielsk (3820) Ostashkov District (6311). Beria, Stalin's secret police chief, in his report to his master, stated that "all officers are uncompromising enemies of the Soviet Union, are anti revolutionists and should be sentenced to death". The Soviet Union had violated the Geneva Convention of 1929 and defied all aspects concerning prisoners of war. Their behaviour was without conscience; it was brutal and despicable.

Thousands of others perished in remote sites, some still unknown. Most were doctors, professors, engineers, teachers, diplomats, civil servants and religious leaders. They were "enemies of the people" to be liquidated in the first phase of the Russian occupation. This was a carefully-prepared plan drawn up and signed by Colonel Serov, Deputy Commissar for Security, to deport the "socially dangerous and anti-Soviet elements" of Polish society. The intelligentsia of Poland were eliminated so that the "simple people" could be exploited more easily as slave labour. The deportees were to be executed or "finished off" in the prisons, forced labour camps and places of enforced settlements in the northern parts of European Russia and Central Asia where extreme conditions would ensure their liquidation. Or so Stalin thought. He did not reckon on the resilience or the faith of the Polish people, especially those of the eastern Borderlands, those "simple people".

There was a small cast-iron stove screwed to the floor

of the wagon, on which we could warm up something to eat, and on one side of the wagon there was just a hole in the middle of the floor for the purposes of hygiene. As it happened my mother needed to use this first, and as usual she solved the problem of decency as efficiently as she solved all other problems. She simply made a screen out of a sheet or bed cover, so everybody used the hole in the floor with some embarrassment, but with enough privacy to hide their blushes. We had candles so we could see in the wagon, but we had no fuel until the guards eventually brought some on one of our many stops and we were then able to cook the provisions we and others had brought with us and share them out amongst us as best we would.

After a couple of days we realised we just had to accept the situation and live with it, as we didn't know how long we were to be in the wagon and couldn't do anything

Journey to prison camp – adapted from a sketch by an unknown artist

about it. In fact we were locked into it, unable to get out, for ten days or more, with stops at intervals to fill with water and coal. At these times we were given buckets of hot water and cabbage soup (lapsza) but you could only drink the water, as the cabbage leaves were inedible. We were given coal and water and some cabbage soup with fishheads floating in it. That too was barely edible, as was the black, sour bread which was handed out at intervals of two or three days.

The condition of the human freight jammed into the cattle trucks defied description. There were about 30 of us squashed into the wagon, and we slept on bunks on straw, while others were on the floor. Deprived of food, warmth and the most basic sanitary requirements, thousands perished during the trip, which was of course the intention. Their bodies were left by the side of the track. It was heartbreaking. Day after day, night after night we heard only the constant moan of the wheels on the tracks picking up speed, taking us further and further away from our country. We passed through villages, fields and forests, all covered in snow. It was bitterly cold and the wagon walls were frozen, our skin freezing to them on contact. In the mornings when we woke we had to prise our clothes away from the walls. We were all in despair, wondering what was going to happen to us. We talked amongst ourselves, we waited for the next move and we prayed and sang patriotic songs and hymns.

Our journey took us through Zdolbunow (February 15th), Iwanko, then passing into Soviet territory at Szepetowka on February 16th, where it was already much colder. We passed through Orzenin, Korosten, Owrucz, Gomel Bryansk and Orze. We went over the river Don and through Karaczew to Aleksandrowka (Feb 21st) to Rybne station. The journey continued through Holworsk and Woskriesensk, and in the early hours of February 23rd we continued to Pokrowa. We eventually passed through Pietruszki and Untow and stopped in the evening of February 23rd at Wlademir. Our next stop was Gorki, where our wagon was detached from the others. We were with the Sieradzkis, Zajdels and others, mostly from the Osada Krechowiecka, and we were, we think, heading north.

We were soon to find out where we were going. After 15 days travelling locked in the wagons we came to the end of the track. We had travelled further northwards and eventually reached a place called Sharya in deepest Russia on February 25th, a journey of over 1000 kilometres. The doors were thrown open and a wilderness of snow stretched before us. So much snow! There were endless wastes of snow, forests and nothing else. It was almost blinding. We were let out, our belongings loaded onto waiting sledges. We looked at each other for reassurance and set off.

We were now forced to march at gunpoint for about 15 kilometres through very deep and heavy snow to the slave labour camps, of which there were two. We were in the furthest. The name of our camp was Posiolek Poldniewica, Szarynskij region, Gorkowskaja Oblast. The nearest city was Gorki, which was over 350 kilometres away.

We learned later that the wagons we had been detached from were headed over the frozen river Volga onward and eastwards.

Portrayal of life in barracks – artist unknown

On our journey we had seen other trains taking Russian 'dissidents' even further into Siberia. Those who had died or fallen were just left piled up on the platforms or by the side of the tracks, their families unable even to cover them to give them some dignity. The thought of leaving loved ones behind in such circumstances must have been unbearable. People can be pushed beyond anger, beyond tears, beyond protest and even beyond grief, until finally you just sink into a dark mire of acceptance, hoping somehow that you will survive.

Finally we reached some wooden barracks which had previously been a prison camp for Latvians (there had always been prison camps throughout Russia for those who had displeased the Russians in some way)

There was a huge gate at the entrance which looked

quite intimidating. It was surrounded by a very tall wooden stockade with guard towers at the corners, and it looked exactly what it was, a prison. We learned later on that the gates were locked only at night, but the guards manned the towers 24 hours a day. The barracks were surrounded by forests which extended for hundreds of kilometres. There was nowhere to run to; escape was futile. We were watched constantly and those who did escape froze to death.

There were 18 barracks, poorly made of very rough wooden logs, and these were to accommodate about 2500 prisoners. The gaps between the logs were stuffed with moss and clay and were full of bugs of all sorts, which feasted on us as we slept. We were sometimes so worn out by our labours that we didn't notice we were being bitten, and we always woke up scratching. There were also many large cracks in the walls through which the cold came, and at times the temperature fell to minus 40 degrees.

We were checked off yet another list, and while some families were packed off into the unknown each family left was allocated a tiny space to live, one family on higher bunks, one on lower bunks. We got our belongings and settled down as best we could. We were with several other families.

There was enough room to lie down, and we slept like sardines, huddling together for warmth and comfort. During the day the bedding was removed and beaten with wooden planks to rid it of as many bugs as possible. It barely made a difference.

The one range stove used for heating and cooking

burned continuously, there being a plentiful supply of wood from the forests. We also used the stove for drying clothes, which were always wet from walking through snow up to our waists, but they were still damp in the morning. The stove chimney was a magnet for cockroaches and other bugs, which absolutely covered it. It is amazing what you learn to live with.

The lack of hygiene due to overcrowding, lack of soap and very primitive toilets (outhouses or slop buckets) was far worse in the summer months. Contaminated water brought a typhoid epidemic and there were many deaths.

The very next day after arriving at the camp, we were sent to work in the forest and were issued with axes and saws. We had only time for a breakfast of balanda, hot water mixed with flour, and a piece of very hard black bread. Not very nourishing, but it had to do. This was now our daily diet, along with 400 grams of slightly less decayed bread. It was freezing, minus 30 degrees, and the Camp Commandant told us "Settle down and work because you'll never get out of here. Hairs will grow on my palms before you leave this place. Forget about Poland, it doesn't exist and never will."

On hearing this we were outraged. We thought "That's what you think." Ziuta, Walery's wife, who was there with her children Marysia and Wlodek, used to stand up to him. She was so small, but she had such determination. When the Amnesty came she reminded him of those words.

We Poles, said Slowacki (a Polish Poet 1831) "must learn to breath underwater", and this stubborn mentality helped us through every wretchedness the Russians threw at us.

In that freezing weather we went to work with our saws and axes, trudging deep into the forest to fell trees in deep snow. It was very difficult for us, as we lived in complete isolation, no radio and no newspapers; we were not even able to talk freely. We did master some Russian in order to get by, to be able to trade what little we had for food.

In Siberia winter came early, in September, and spring came late, in May. We had to work as teams and my father and I were a team. Everybody above 16, or those considered big enough and strong enough - this included Wlodek, who was 15 - had to work in order to eat. Here in Russia this was the rule - if you didn't work you didn't eat. The under-16s, including Jasia, Janusz and Marysia, went to the camp school to learn Russian.

Day after day at six o'clock in the morning we had to get up and wade into deep snow up to our knees and in places our waists, to fell trees. The men would cut the trees down while the younger people removed the branches and stacked them into big piles ready for the horses to drag them away on wagons to the depot. There was a sawmill here with electrical saws and generators. Men worked in groups cutting railway sleepers or props and pit stops. The younger men and women cut wood into slices with electric saws and fed them into a machine which cut them into cubes, which were used for fuel in the substation. There were many accidents, as it was difficult to use these tools with frozen hands and there wasn't medical or nursing help at the camp. Many people died from infections to their wounds.

We were not paid for many months and the rations barely sustained us. Finally, the Russians began to pay us for our hard work. The wages were very low, just a few roubles, but it helped us to buy some goods from the nearby villages. We were forbidden to have any contact with the local people, but hunger forced us to break the rules. The Commandant mostly overlooked this in the beginning, as he realised he needed us to be strong enough to work and meet the deadlines imposed on him from headquarters.

We worked at backbreaking jobs. Some of us were sent to collective farms or mines, while others slaved in the

Arrival at camp – adapted from a drawing by an unknown artist

quarries. We worked in the forests, felling trees regardless of our fitness and health, braving the most inhumane climatic conditions so that the Russians could continue the railway track that had ended at Sharya, where we had got off the train. They intended to build deeper into Siberia, one can only assume to give easier access to other labour camps and the gulags.

Some of the more able and experienced men were given the responsibility of building new barracks. They worked very hard for slightly better wages and larger rations of bread. These projects were usually completed in very good time, as accommodation was needed for newer intakes of prisoners.

The days were long, from early morning till late at night. If we were lucky my mother would give us hot water with maybe raspberry twigs that she'd foraged for during the day. They didn't have much taste, but they took the edge off the hunger pangs. She also managed to find mushrooms. There was very little else to eat, maybe a little stale bread. Those who couldn't work in the forests, like my mother, spent most of the day cleaning the beds and the living areas.

The primitive barracks, stables and chicken huts where we lived were infested with bugs, cockroaches, lice and fleas, which were eating us alive, though the bunks were scrubbed down with scalding water each day. Life was so very difficult to endure.

There was a small village about three kilometres from the camp and the villagers, mostly Russian 'dissidents', were very kind to us. They held markets on occasion and we were able to buy or barter for much-needed food from them. At the last moment before boarding the sledge to leave Rowne, Kazia had grabbed as many scarves, handerchiefs and other small items as she could knowing they would probably exchange well.

These Russians had been exiled from their homeland after the Russian revolution of 1917. Like us they had been given no notice. They had just been physically removed from their homes, loaded onto transport and brought to this wasteland to work on collective farms. They were not even able to take any possessions with them, so they had arrived with absolutely nothing but the clothes they stood up in. They were then expected to build their own homes and work for their Russian masters, sending a great proportion of their farm goods to them and surviving on very little. Yet they were able to help us. They were so kind, especially the older generation, who could probably empathise with what we were experiencing.

There were many good Russians, but the communists soon filtered these out and disposed of them, either to the Gulags or collective farms across the vast wilderness of Russia. These older Russians couldn't even be open with their children, who would report them to the authorities for any outspoken comments. Their children had been indoctrinated from early school age into the ideals of communism, so they knew no other doctrine.

One old Russian had become friendly with Adam and they were able to chat to each other (there are many

Adapted from a drawing by Sobierajski

similarities between the Russian and Polish languages) on several occasions. They were both very much against communism, but they had to be so careful what they talked about as the NKVD jumped on the slightest anti-communist remark as being almost treasonable.

The village markets soon stopped, probably because we were getting too friendly, which of course would not be tolerated by the Russians. We had to be very aware of what we said and did from then on. Maybe we had been careless and had been overheard saying something completely innocuous but considered anti-communist.

There were two occasions during our time in the labour camps when we experienced absolute terror. The first took place in our billet in Duraszewo camp, where there lived three families, us, another Polish family and a family from the Ukraine. The Ukrainians weren't very fond of us Poles, nor were we of them, and they more often than not worked with the Russians to gain special favours. The atmosphere at times was tense and we wondered if they had been put amongst us to spy on us. Extreme hunger affects the mind in a very negative way.

During our incarceration we tried very hard to keep our spirits up. Sometimes we sang and danced, and we were singing one evening when all of a sudden the door opened and the Commandant stood there with his rifle and dog and told Adam to go with him. It wasn't the usual evening head count, when guards came with their dogs. We all froze. So many men had been taken by the Commandant for interrogation and were never seen again. We didn't know why he was there and were terrified thinking about what might happen.

All of a sudden the Commandant seemed to change his mind. He just turned on his heel and walked out without saying a word. He never mentioned the incident again. To us it was a miracle.

We later learned that the father of the Ukrainian family had sent his son to the Commandant to tell him that Adam had been making fun of the Russians, which was completely untrue and just malicious. We were even more alert after that and the Ukrainian father was a little more hostile, as his spiteful effort to gain any indulgence from the guards hadn't worked.

The other incident happened in Derewalka camp when we had completely run out of food. All available food was being diverted to the Russian army, which at that time was fighting against the Germans. Kazia couldn't feed us and the Commandant wouldn't issue any more passes to enable us to go out to the villages to barter for food. We were so very close to starvation and struggled for energy to complete our chores. Food had been very scarce anyway, but this was far worse.

Sofia, Kazia's mother, had been able to send us parcels and we had been able to exchange letters, heavily censored of course, with her for a little while. It was such a comfort to keep in touch, and to know that she had so far survived, as she was now quite elderly. All parcels and letters were sent to the regional Post Office, which was about 15 kilometres from the camp. We had to collect them, walking through muddy country roads and fields and in winter in very deep snow, which made it so very difficult. It usually took a day there and back and Jasia and Janusz used to go together, with Marysia tagging along sometimes. They often didn't get back to camp until after dark, absolutely exhausted but so happy with their packages, although sometimes they were empty-handed and despondent.

All this stopped very suddenly; no letters, no contact, no parcels of desperately-needed food. We later found that they had been confiscated by the NKVD, which wasn't a surprise. We never found out what had happened to Sofia. After the war it was very difficult to find out anything about anyone's family, as the Russians put a complete block on information and communication. It wasn't in the best interests of the new communist state of Poland!

One evening after work Adam, in desperation, made the decision to take Kazia's wedding ring (his had already been bartered) and despite his emaciated state, set off for one of the nearest villages, which was several kilometres away. My father was not a man to make hasty decisions. He was a quietly confident and reserved man, not inclined to be rushed into impulsive behaviour or to putting his life or that of his family in danger, but we were slowly starving. We were struggling to maintain our work commitments, and "if you don't work you don't eat" was the Russian principle. We could not go on much longer; we had to survive.

It had snowed, but not heavily, and was still quite light. Adam set off in determined mood and reached the village, where he was able to exchange the ring for potatoes and flour. He was exhausted, as the trek to the village had taken a lot out of him, but he had to get back.

He had only been going for a short time when it started to snow quite heavily, and he lost his way completely. Everything looked the same, and all he could see was a wall of white, swirling snow. He was desperate - this time the Commandant wouldn't be so lenient, he thought.

He couldn't go any further. He couldn't see a thing - no path, nothing but a blanket of snow. He stopped, gathered his thoughts, said some prayers, and got down to collecting some kindling from under the beech trees and bushes. The kindling was still fairly dry at that stage, and he was able to light a fire, although it took some time as his fingers were almost frozen. He then squatted down by the flames. He did not know how long he sat there in total despair, clinging onto his sack of food, wondering if he'd see his family again or if the wolves would get him. Which way should he go? He had no idea. He was so tired, so cold and so hungry, and he was becoming disorientated. He thought it was hopeless. How would he get back? What should he do? Oh how he needed Kazia, his rock. Had he told her he loved her recently?

He cried until he shook. He just wanted to sleep. How had he got into this nightmare? How could he get out of it?

The snow was falling steadily around him as he sat there and he still couldn't see any landmarks, let alone a path. He prayed as he'd never prayed before in his life for a miracle, a way back to his family.

The Poles were so deeply attached to their religion that it brought them through the nightmare. Praying had given Adam what he needed, an incentive.

All of a sudden, with what little strength he had left, he got up, his mind absolutely set. He had decided on a direction. He put aside his hunger and weariness and started walking. He walked as if his life depended on it, one foot in front of the other, that's all he had to do. His body was beyond exhaustion. He was soaked by the snow, which had got through to his skin, and so very cold. His hands could barely keep hold of his precious goods, but he was determined about one thing - to get back to the camp. His family was waiting for him. It was a major effort and every muscle cried out for rest.

After what seemed like hours, he arrived back at the gates of the camp, where the Commandant stood with his rifle and dog by a large fire. The fire was like a magnet, drawing him ever closer to where he really shouldn't be. Should he not go round the side of the camp? Try getting in another way? But it was surrounded by wide open spaces and the forests were so far away. So many escapees had never made it; they had just disappeared. And he was so tired. He felt resigned to his fate. His legs shook and were about to give way.

"Goral, where have you been?" said the Commandant, and Adam answered, so close to tears, the adrenalin taking over, "I had to go for food for my family, they are starving, I had no choice, you left me no choice".

"We'll talk about it in the morning" was the response from the Commandant, and he went through the gates back into the camp, leaving Adam just standing there, exhausted almost to the point of collapse, not sure what to do next. Kazia had been watching out for his return. She ran out and grabbed him, pulling him back into their barracks. We children were still awake, curled up on the bunk together waiting to see what had happened. We couldn't sleep, how could we sleep? We'd kept as quiet as we could so as not to alarm the guards, and after keeping our feelings in for so long we burst into tears. We were so relieved to see him.

Adam still held the potatoes and flour; he had never let go of them. Kazia had to prize the sack away from his frozen hands before throwing a blanket over him. We would never forget the dread we had felt that night. There were many occasions over the first few years of my new life in England when I would very suddenly be reminded of these times. They just crept into my thoughts without warning and would leave me in a state of panic for some time. I still think of them occasionally, but without the awful panic.

In spite of everything, the Commandant seemed to have a conscience. He had been kind to us on two occasions. After the signing of the Amnesty he simply vanished into the night with his wife and dog. Where could they have gone to find safety? Or had he been sent to fight the Germans?

Adam had risked his life, but for a very good reason, to keep us all alive. He had seen what was happening to us, what physical state we were in. We had lost a great deal of weight, and we were wasting away in front of him. Our muscles ached so much it was painful to move. We couldn't lift the heavy saws to cut the trees and we were anaemic, lethargic, dehydrated. Our skin was becoming cracked, we were so fatigued, how could we work? It was far worse for Kazia, this was having a dire effect on her heart and she was struggling to get through each day despite her determination.

Aunty Ziuta also risked her life, although in a different way. She was very outspoken, which may seem insignificant, but the words she aimed at the Russians and Ukranian guards could have had enormous impact. She too escaped with her life. She was only a very small woman, but with a massive heart and personality. What delight could a snarling NKVD guard possibly take from responding harshly to the insults of such a small person, a non-person? What bravado could he have gained in the barracks in front of his colleagues? The sheer strength of human spirit and unbreakable bond between us got us through unimaginable privations.

After the snow melted we had to dig deep into the ground, which was clay and very wet, to make way for the laying of the railway tracks. We were standing in deep water digging and digging all day and coming back to the barracks cold and wet and tired for something to eat, and of course there was very little and we usually went to bed hungry. We had by then finished the food Adam had risked his life for, sharing it out as carefully as we could. We lay close together for warmth and comfort, holding tight. At times there was no bread because no food was delivered. If we had any clothing to exchange for food, we would go to the vilage of the collective farm (the Kolkhozy), where we were able to get some potatoes or flour so that my mother could cook something for us workers in the family, but this had now come to an end, the Commandant having put a stop to our visits. We had very little to eat throughout, usually just a piece of bread and a drink of tea made of raspberry twigs. We cleaned our teeth with charcoal powder. There was no tea or coffee, so we drank a brew made of acorns and called it coffee. In the summer months, however, we could sustain ourselves with berries and mushrooms, which were plentiful.

Winters were very bad, with temperatures falling to minus 40. Snow fell often and the frost was bitter. We had been given padded trousers and anoraks filled with wool and wore shoes made from wicker, and around our legs we wrapped strips of woollen pieces from our shoes to our knees. They were very light and warm if wrapped around properly. Life was very sad and very hard, and could be demoralising, but we youngsters amused ourselves after work even on an empty stomach by singing hopeful songs and praying when we could. Praying in groups wasn't allowed. Day after day we hoped and prayed that some time soon, somebody would rescue us from this inhuman land. Did anybody know we were there? Perhaps no one knew we had been deported. What was happening back home

The guards were very cruel; they would come around each night for roll call with their dogs. Roll call was at a

Adapted from a drawing by an unknown artist

different time each night to try and catch us out, to keep us constantly on alert. They didn't physically mistreat us too harshly, as they needed us to work for them, but they abused us verbally. If a girl happened to be pretty she would be singled out for attention, but fathers kept a keen eye on their daughters. We youngsters were able to accept the situation more easily than our parents, who were very depressed, only waiting for the day when we would be free again. To think of escape was impossible, as there were always guards and dogs. The camp was surrounded by wide open spaces and then the forests which very few made it to. Kazia and Adam, although quite subdued, never gave up hope; somehow they knew we would be free, that we would survive. They never doubted it. Accidents, starvation and sickness took its toll on the prisoners, but the most distressing cause of death was psychological causes. Anyone who lost faith in survival did not last more than a few days. It was quite unnerving.

After about 12 months in the camp at Poldniewica, we were moved to a smaller camp, Duraszewo, which was about four kilometres away. We were sent with four other families and had to work as hard as we had done before, on even poorer rations and in even worse conditions. Amongst them were the family Krawiec, Bruno and Maryan, their sisters Krysia and Irena and their parents.

Bruno and his brother Maryan later fought at Monte Cassino and I still see Bruno and his wife Halina to this day. Halina had lost her parents in Russia, where they had succumbed to the privations. As orphans, she and her two brothers and four sisters were sent to Africa. Of all the groups of Polish children leaving Persia via different routes to various places of refuge, the largest went to Africa. This was the move most feared, especially by the women guardians, who were concerned about the unhealthy climate, wild animals and so on. They were worried that the last remnants of the children's strength would be exhausted. The military families used all their influence to delay the departure or avoid it entirely. The first group ready for departure rebelled, such was their agitation, and British soldiers surrounded the camp in Teheran to ensure that nobody could leave. Resistance eventually abated and transports began to leave for Africa.

Winter was soon coming again and we were moved yet again to camp Derewalka. The first snow fell early, and it was very frosty and food was becoming even scarcer. Many had died through starvation. What clothing we had left was exchanged for potatoes, but that was all. The Commandant had relented and allowed us to visit the villages again for food, but the villagers by then also had very little to barter for as they were stockpiling for another hard winter and couldn't afford to let us have very much. There were so many of us wanting food. Day followed day and life went by and we continued to work, although with great difficulty, felling trees and building the railway line further into Siberia and our health was still a matter for great concern.

One day whilst I was cutting branches off a tree and putting them onto a bonfire I noticed a young man sitting on a fallen tree with our foreman, watching me. When we finished work and my father and I were walking to the barracks, the young man walked along with us. We talked, and when I got to the barracks he told me he was a member

One of the many burials endured by parents of a child who could not survive the utter deprivation of life in Siberia

of a young communist party (Comsomolts) and that he would come and see me again. My father, still very watchful, called me in then. It could have been a very difficult situation. We didn't want to antagonise the guards but we also didn't want to encourage any friendships either, especially those of a romantic nature, as this might have led to an even worse situation.

The young man did come again several times to our barracks and each time he brought a balalaika and played for me, and I don't even remember his name. My father wasn't happy that he was seeing me and did his best to quietly discourage him. The last time he came he very solemnly told me he loved me but that he had to go to war. I never saw him again. This young Russian was the very first man who told me he loved me.

Soon after that we started being left to our own devices. There was hardly any bread and anything else was inedible, and we heard that everything was now being sent to the front for the soldiers. The guards seemed restless, and we sensed something was happening. One day, June 22nd 1941, we found that the guards with their dogs had left the camps. They had just disappeared overnight. News filtered through from some of the villagers who had been watching from the outskirts of the camp until it was safe to come in that Germany had declared war on Russia, and we began to hope that things might change.

The absurdity of the situation was that we were saved by our other aggressor Hitler and his attack on Russia. Mr Churchill had persuaded Stalin to release all Polish prisoners to allow them to fight against the Nazis and in fact become allies to Russia! Russia, now with German troops deep in her territories, re-established diplomatic relations with the Polish Government in exile in London. The Soviet Union, on orders from Churchill in Britain, agreed to grant an amnesty to all Polish citizens who had been forcibly deprived of their freedom and taken to Russia. When this news came through to us, we were elated.

Although emaciated by disease and exhausted from the harshness of the life we had led, we survivors made our way in our hundreds of thousands from the most remote corners of Russia out of the camps and towards freedom and our countrymen. We were to leave behind so many of our number, buried in crude graves and those too exhausted and aged and worn down by starvation to be able to make a journey of any distance, even if it meant freedom.

These poor people were skeletal, wearing only rags, their feet covered in paper. They were so very thin, as we were, but they looked old and wrinkled. They were bloated and their skin was yellow, their eyes sunken. They were so weak some of them couldn't stand up. There were not enough of us who were strong enough to help them and they had to be left behind. It was heart-breaking.

General Sikorsky, on behalf of the Polish Government, signed the first diplomatic agreement on 30th July 1941. The Soviet Ambassador to Britain, Maisky, then announced that the Soviet-Nazi Germany treaty of August 1939 relating to the territorial division of Poland along the Ribbentrop-Molotov Line was no longer valid. This agreement also included a special statement concerning Polish prisoners of war and Polish civilian deportees in the USSR. Stalin promised to release Polish prisoners of war and the huge number of us deportees who had been exiled to Siberia. In Russia there were almost 200.000 POWs, who were released and allowed to form a Polish army in Russia. When Stalin cut off their supplies in 1942 they were evacuated to the Middle East.

That winter the German forces reached Moscow and Leningrad. Here their advance was halted by the Siberian-trained Russian enforcements, which were better prepared for the severe winter than the Germans, who were surrounded and slaughtered mercilessly. Captured Germans were either shot on the spot or deported to Siberia, where most perished.

At about this time relations between Stalin and the Polish Government deteriorated over disagreements over the borderlands between the eastern provinces, Stalin insisting they should be absorbed into the Soviet Union after the war. Vyacheslav Molotov, Soviet Foreign Secretary, was in London to press the case for the territories of Poland and the Baltic states, formerly carved up by Hitler and Stalin. Stalin now wanted the Allies to endorse this same deal. The British Government thought this utterly immoral and Churchill refused, only granting a general treaty of alliance and no promise of any territory. This was overturned at Yalta, Stalin had his territories and the Iron Curtain came down on Eastern Europe. At the same time, after the Pearl Harbour massacre of USA personnel and the large-scale destruction of ships, planes and equipment by Japanese bombers on 7th November 1941, America finally entered the war.

Stalin had put us in those camps to work us to death, and if it hadn't been for the amnesty, when Russia had become an ally of the British and Americans, he might have succeeded. Our history shows us Russia's greed for our land, to expand the Russian Empire even further and seek revenge for past uprisings. Our hostile feelings towards the Russians were returned in full.

To someone who does not know the Russians it would seem that all of Russia's cruel hostility against Poland would cease when she became Poland's ally against Germany, especially when, with the treaty of July 1941, the Polish army was formed on Russian territories to increase forces against a common enemy, Germany. Russia had no intention of giving up the eastern territories she had seized at the beginning of the war. Stalin's aim was to dominate all of Poland and turn her into a communist state, and it was clear from the Yalta conference that the Allies would not oppose Stalin's plans, and that Roosevelt had again given in to him.

It would appear that Roosevelt, especially, had throughout the war given in to Stalin time and time again, thinking he could control him and so ensure a peaceful resolution and keep America out of the conflict. Roosevelt had very cleverly funded both Britain and Russia to fight the war for him, despite Churchill's many pleas to actively enter the battle. The US president seems to have preferred to pull the strings, making most of the decisions that would affect millions of people in peacetime. It was only when the Japanese attacked Pearl Harbour in 1941 that America actively entered the war.

Since the partition of Poland at the Yalta Convention in 1945, our home town of Rowne has been part of the Ukraine. In February of that year at the Yalta Conference, Roosevelt and Churchill confirmed what had already been discussed and agreed with Stalin (without Polish representation or that of any other occupied country) about the existing annexation of the eastern half of Poland. Three old men decided the fate of millions - a bloodthirsty tyrant, a terminally-ill statesman who knew little of the real issues, and Churchill, who we felt had abandoned us. The agreement had consigned Poland to the "Soviet sphere of influence" and for many Poles to return to their homeland meant death or another trip to Siberia. Many settled in the UK, USA, Canada, France, South America and several other countries. Unless you were a communist, there was no future in Poland.

Although Germany was beaten and the Allies won the war, we Poles were the real losers. Over half a million fighting men and women and six million civilians died, over 22% of the population. About 50% of these were Polish Christian and 50% Polish Jews. Approximately 5,384,000 (90%) of the Polish war losses (Jews and Gentiles) were the victims of prisons, death camps, executions, annihilation of ghettos, epidemics, starvation, excessive work and ill treatment. So many Poles were sent to concentration camps that virtually every family had someone close to it who had been tortured or murdered there.

There were one million war orphans and over half a million invalids. The country lost 38% of its national assets (Britain lost 0.8%, France 1.5%) and half the country was swallowed up by the Soviet Union, including the two great cultural centres of Lwow and Wilno. So many had died in the camps, of disease, bad water, mosquitoes, ill treatment and starvation. They had been worked to death and told they would never leave. When we buried our dead in the mud, under little mounds of earth, singing our patriotic songs, some of the coffins lay on the water because of the high water table, and it was so dirty. Yet so many did survive, mostly by simply believing they would. They had their sheer determination and their Catholic faith to get through. They had indeed learned to breathe under water.

HOPELESS AND HOMELESS

Now that an amnesty had been proclaimed for all Poles in the territories of the Soviet Union, we were free to go. There was great joy. Discharge documents had to be arranged, and there was much to do and to think about. But our joy was followed by a new worry - after two years of homelessness, where were we to go? We had to go somewhere, we needed a place to head to, we had to move. Only in flight could safety lie.

General Anders, our military leader, was freed from the notorious Lubianka prison in Moscow and news reached us that the Polish army was reforming under his command in the Middle East, with some units being formed within the Soviet Union. Everyone wanted to join the Polish army. We knew what we had to do, but not how to do it.

After the amnesty had been declared, Uncle Walery had walked into the camp. We didn't recognise him. He was very badly bruised and thin and gaunt, with long hair and dirty clothes and a beard down to his chest. Yet somehow, he had found us - he always managed to find us. He had been caught on the western border taking his sister Genia and her daughter Halina to her husband Wladislaw in Lublin. He had been coming back to collect his own family when he had been caught by the NKVD. He had been accused of being a spy and transported to a prison at Swierdlowski, in the salt mines in the Urals, where General Anders had also been imprisoned. He had also been tortured, for no reason whatsoever.

Ziuta had found out where he was and she was able to write to him to make sure he knew where we were so that some contact could be maintained. Despite such isolation, no papers, no radio, contact was always somehow made. Word was always able to get through, although it did take some time.

Genia, Wladislaw and their daughter Halina stayed in Lublin and survived the war, somehow managing to avoid the atrocities. Other relatives remained in German-occupied western Poland, in Lodz. Some survived, but some of the male members were imprisoned, and two of Adam's brothers-in-law were trapped in a prison set alight by the Germans, and perished there.

Our camps, Poldniewica, Derawalka and Duraszowo, elected a representative who would go to the HQ for more information and advice about what to do with our newly-gained freedom and how to progress to the next stage of our journey. We needed to know what to do now we were able to travel freely.

A few days later a telegram arrived at the camp from

the Polish Embassy in Kuybishev. It said that all officers, soldiers and all those who are able to serve were asked to report to the nearest HQ of the Soviet Army, from where they would be directed to the new Polish Army. All Soviet authorities had the correct information. Those who reported would receive the necessary travel documents and food stamps.

We elected Antoni Maj as our representative and he visited the Polish embassy in Kuybyshev, named after the Bolshevik leader Valerian Kuybyshev who took the city in the October revolution of 1917. It is the administrative centre of Samara, and a major river port situated at the junction of the Volga and Samara rivers in close view of the Zhiguli mountains. In 1941 the prospect of Moscow falling to the invading Germans seemed so likely that it was chosen to be the new capital of Russia. The Communist party and governmental organisations, diplomats and leading cultural establishments were evacuated to the city. As history shows, the Russians defeated the Germans and most of the area's 1.5 million Germans were dispersed into exile or to forced labour camps. In 1991 the city was given back its historical name of Samara.

Antoni returned some days later bearing a certificate from the Embassy officially nominating him as a spokesman for us refugees. I remember when Antoni got back and told us we were free to go where we wanted - it was the happiest day of our lives. What joy and relief!

The Polish Ambassador to the USSR, Stanislaw Kot,

and his small team had the enormous task of organising relief for the hundreds of thousands of Poles dispersed throughout the vastness of the Soviet Union. The first task was to find them, as they were spread over such a wide area. The delegates were to set up orphanages, feeding centres, hospitals and schools throughout Russia for all who had been released from the labour camps and exile and to somehow get us all to where the Polish Army was being formed. Embassy delegates were sent all over Russia to arrange this massive programme of relief.

It took some time to organise the necessary papers (the amnesty document which would serve as the family passport and as a one way travel permit to the destination of our choice) and transport from Kirow, and Antoni, with several able assistants, was working so hard to organise everything. How he accomplished it all is a mystery. Transport was to be arranged for our entire community to go south east, as a Polish army was being formed in Buzuluk, in the southern Ural Mountains. General Wladyslaw Anders, commander of the Polish Army, had set up his headquarters there. Without the papers we would again be faced with hunger, as the papers entitled us to soup and bread at various station canteens. However my father's papers were withheld, because of his outspoken views on communism and his previous military history, so we couldn't leave. We were in absolute despair. What were we to do?

There were four or five other families like us who couldn't leave for the same reason. My father, together with men from the other families who were denied the necessary papers, hated everything that communism represented and perhaps foolishly, considering the company they were in, they were not afraid to say so. He and the others were also considered 'social undesirables' for their part in the Uprising of 1920. So when all around us were busily getting ready to leave we were being held back. How the records of the men in question, their military history and political views had got into the hands of the authorities we never found out, but as a rule the Russians were able to find out information about everyone. They had their methods!

The Russian authorities went out of their way to postpone the departure, as they were determined to keep their slave labourers as long as possible, and at the last moment they refused to allocate a train. However, a few days later Antoni was successful and he acquired one.

The transport for the others had been organised and was now waiting, and we still were not able to leave with them. I cannot describe our feelings of hopelessness. We were absolutely desperate; how we wept.

Our prayers were answered, for yet another good Samaritan appeared on our side. Just as the train was about to leave, Antoni arrived with our papers so that we could leave with the others. We were at last free to go. We didn't know how Antoni had got the discharge papers, but we didn't care. We couldn't believe that at last we were leaving the labour camps behind.

Although we were free to go for the time being, there

was still a lot of hardship to endure before we were truly free. Some families stayed behind by choice they were White Russians or Ukrainians, those who had communist sympathies, although no one knew how they would survive in that inhospitable land.

We got our few scraps together, including the most precious photo albums, hugged each other, and with many others set off to Kotlas with lighter hearts and great determination. Those that could walk did so, while others were in horse-drawn wagons or arbas. We were to travel in cattle transports again, but we were not being watched or tormented by the communist guards. Food was always scarce, even now, but we were happy because we were moving away from the dreaded labour camps, going south towards Bukhara in Uzbekistan and away from Stalin's grip. Our hearts were lighter.

At Kotlas we were allocated a space and the train moved onto Kirow, where there were many hundreds more people waiting on the platform. Some were able to board, but others were left to wait for the next transport. People sometimes waited many days for a train, vulnerable to the weather and thieves. We were very often shunted onto a side rail to wait, as other transports carrying military equipment were given priority.

Being classified as military transport enabled us to receive small rations of soup, bread and boiled water, and we had to show our identification papers to get this. The journey from Kirow to Bukhara, which was our destination, was over 5000 kilometres, and we braced ourselves for a very long and gruelling journey.

At Kirow, one of the main stations on the trans-Siberian route, we were able to get out and stretch our legs but were very aware that the train could leave the station without any warning. Many people were caught out by this and were separated from their families, never to see them again.

We were heading towards the Ural Mountains and had to change trains many times, as there were hundreds of us and the trains were very crowded. They were also very unreliable, as we were to find out. Some of the routes were guarded by a network of spies and the NKVD, who only worsened the evacuation process by relocating thousands of Soviet citizens at the same time. This was a deliberate ploy to cause us as much difficulty as possible and an attempt by the NKVD to resettle as many deportees in the poorest part of Turkestan they could. They thrived on creating problems for others, but they failed, as so many determined Poles managed to get through to other southern republics of Russia.

We spent our time watching the countryside go by, sharing thoughts with others, sometimes just lost in our thoughts, thinking of home and wondering if we would ever see it again. At times we just huddled together to give each other comfort and the confidence to go on. Kazia always had a word of comfort or humour to keep us going. She truly was the glue that held us all together.

After many days travelling, through the most beautiful landscapes of forests, valleys, rivers and mountain ridges, we arrived at Swierdlowsk. This time we were able to get out at regular intervals and speak to our friends from other wagons and see the happy faces of people who didn't seem to have a care in the world for the first time in two years. We'd been travelling for several long and very uncomfortable days, always hungry, and it was very hot and dusty, but it didn't seem to matter, at least, not at first. But there was still terrible hardship to follow. At some stops, we had seen armed men guarding mounds of salt and huge piles of wheat. Salt was sold on the black market by the matchbox-full at a very high price. At other stops we saw men with horse-drawn carts collecting the corpses of those who had died of starvation and illness.

Jasia, Janusz and I took the opportunity to explore Swierdlowsk, as we had been assured that the train had to refuel and take on provisions and would not be leaving until the next morning. There were many buildings and beautiful monuments along the streets, one of Catherine the Great, but we were too tired and too hot to really enjoy the sights so we headed back to the station.

As we approached the station we saw a very long train filled with Germans who we heard had been rounded up from German communities across Russia, perhaps from Kuybyshev. They were probably being transported to the camps we had come from. Their cries for food and water were desperate, but we couldn't help them. The doors to the wagons were closed. We saw many such transports of human misery heading into Russia.

We quickly ran for our wagon and climbed on. This frightened us, as it immediately brought back memories of our journey into Russia. We left Swierdlowsk in the morning, heading for Chelabinsk 250 kilometres away, and then Aktubinsk an even longer journey of 1670 kilometres. We changed trains there for Oktiabrsk, a shorter journey of 102 kilometres. These had been very long, arduous journeys, so far over 3000 kilometres. It was very hot and we were filthy and exhausted and had lost track of time. The shortage of food and the unwashed bodies and clothes were irritants, but we were together and safer.

The train rumbled on to Shalkar and the Aral Sea, now on the Trans-Aral railway, and finally, after a journey of about six weeks and a total of over 5000 kilometres, we arrived in Tashkent, capital of Uzbekistan. It was a drab and very old station, still marked with the Turkish moon and star. We were all exhausted, hungry and filthy. We sat on the platform, talked to friends, looked for food and waited.

This had been a most fatiguing journey and very many didn't make it despite their determination. Worn down by starvation, typhus, dysentery and malaria and with no energy left to go on, they just dropped. We'd be chatting to our friends one day and the next morning they didn't wake up

After several hours we boarded another train, stopping first at Samarkand, a journey of 300 kilometres, and after another 200 kilometres we reached Bukhara, where we all left the train. We said our goodbyes to our friends, including the Krawiec family, Bruno, Maryjan and their sisters Kryzia and Irena and their parents.

Many years later I became friendly with a Polish woman, Halina, while I was taking my younger son Chris to junior school in Birmingham and she was taking her daughter Elizbeth. She invited me to her home once and I noticed her wedding photograph. I said "I recognise that woman" and Halina said "but how can you, she's my mother in law?" Just then a tall dark man walked into the lounge and we recognised each other immediately. He was Bruno from the family Krawiec, to whom we had said goodbye back in 1942 in Bukhara. How can you hold back tears when such vivid memories suddenly overwhelm you? We remain friends to this day.

During our journey south we had suffered many hardships, but we had held on to the hope that the Polish army would be there to protect us at the end. It was quite a shock then when leaving the train at Bukhara we were told to get our belongings and carry them to a field, where we were to camp for a short time. There was no sign of the Polish army and no one knew where it was located.

We had been allocated different places from the Krawieces by our representative, Antoni. This was sad, because we had become very friendly and each family tended to cling very tight to any friends they made.

The Uzbek authorities had decided to send us to collective farms. Next day we were given arbas (trucks), pulled by mules, for our belongings, and we had to walk with many other families about ten kilometres to a place called Vapkent. It was the middle of the night, but at least we didn't have deep snow. We had to spend another night in the open but it was early autumn and still quite mild. There were four small huts and nothing to eat, but we were used to this and just gritted our teeth. We didn't know where we were. It was so dark and we couldn't see a thing.

We were in Uzbekistan, the site of one of the world's oldest civilised regions. An ancient Persian province, it was conquered by Alexander the Great and the Nomads, Arabs and Turks over the centuries. From the 4th century BC to the 16th century AD Bukhara and Tashkent, situated as they were on the major trade routes to China, India, Persia and Europe, were centres of prosperity, culture and wonderful luxury. The Uzbeks invaded in the 16th century and extended the domain over parts of Persia and Chinese Turkistan. The empire then began to break up into separate principalities, one being Bukhara. Sorely weakened by warfare, these were conquered by Russian forces who took Tashkent in 1865 and Bukhara in 1868. These regions then became vassal states of Russia and after prosperity, peace and luxury came communism, domination and poverty.

There were now very many of us gathered, waiting for someone to tell us where to go, and we had a very unsettled night. When morning came we were told we were being sent to the Kolkhozy, a little village and a collective farm. After many patient hours of waiting several wagons appeared, arbas with mules driven by quite wild-looking men. They wore black fur hats and were nomads. They got off their carts and through gestures told the weaker ones to get on board the arbas. Only my mother was allowed to ride, and those like her who were too weak or too ill to walk. Fortunately this time it was only five kilometres or so and the stronger ones of us set off.

By lunchtime we still hadn't eaten. We reached the Kolkhozy, which was in very barren countryside, with clouds of dust everywhere. It filled our eyes, our mouths and noses and made us cough and almost choke. We were taken to a big clay hut with an open fire in the middle, full of smoke and with a group of people with strange faces looking curiously at us. We had never seen an Uzbek before, and the Uzbeks had never seen a European before. They were strong sturdy people, with broad yellow faces, flat noses, very prominent cheek bones and cool dark eyes. We just watched each other. It was a strange meeting, but despite our differences, especially in appearance, they were friendly towards us. They would need us to work for them!

Early evening came and we were so hungry. We were given some uruk - dried fruit - to eat, for which we were very grateful. Our diet from then was frozen turnips and linseed cakes, cattle feed, which was tasteless and indigestible. Then each family was allocated a kibitka, a

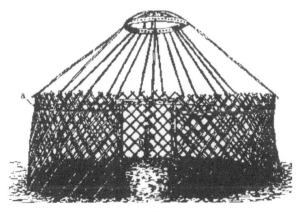

a kibitka

tent of the nomad Uzbek tribes, also known as a yurta, where we had to sleep. They had no lights and no beds or furnishings. The huts were fashioned from home-made clay and bricks mixed with straw, and the roofs were either thatched or tiled with a hole in the middle. The village foreman managed to get us some boards and straw, so we had something to make beds with.

We were soon at work again, organised by the village master of the collective farm. He came to our kibitka in the morning and asked us to follow him into the fields, where he explained what we had to do. This time the work involved digging irrigation canals and carrying soil from one place to another to level the ground for the cotton fields. It was work far beyond our strength, but if we didn't work we didn't receive the dhzugara, similar to wheat, our 'payment'. The younger people picked cotton in the fields. Even infants were taken by their mothers to earn their 'payment'.

Watering was done by irrigation, and the ground had to be level for the water to be transferred from one place to another. We did this from morning to evening. The land, had once been known for its riches, but through communism and collective farming it had suffered poverty and severe hunger. Before the October Revolution of 1917 it had been regarded as a paradise.

Throughout our journey towards the Middle East we were dependent upon others for our survival, but we had not expected to exchange one slavery for another, becoming unpaid and mostly unfed workers for the Soviet collective system! We worked from sunrise to sunset for a handful of flour. There was no fruit or vegetables. We grew thinner and weaker, as there was not enough to nourish us. Complete families were being wiped out through starvation, malaria and dysentery.

We didn't receive much help from the Polish authorities at that time as they were so far stretched organising the evacuation of so very many thousands of us from such a vast area. We did at times meet some delegates from the Polish Embassy on the roads recruiting personnel from amongst us deportees to help with the organisation.

The Russians refused to help us in any way; in fact they went out of their way to disrupt everything they possibly could. The trains, trucks and food were now being diverted to serve the needs of the Russian army while we were left to starve. We had to work for our daily bread again. The amount of food we received was dependent on the weight of cotton we picked or the number of heaps of soil we had moved, 70 being the required quota. We were given maize flour and sometimes dried fruit, again only so much per working person. It wasn't much and we didn't always get it. Again we were hungry because there wasn't enough to eat, and at times there wasn't any flour, so my mother picked some weeds and boiled them for us so that we had something to eat. Jasia and I were the workers and Kazia and Janusz searched for herbs, sorrel, anything edible. Things were getting desperate yet again. Would we ever eat a proper meal, would our hunger ever go away?

By this time we had heard that the Polish army was being formed, and word had got round that families who had a member in the army had a better chance of getting out of these inhumane conditions. They would be allowed to go to the Middle East, where the army was gathering. Thinking their families would be all right, Adam, Uncle Walery and others had left us to go and enlist in Uzbekistan. But it wasn't to be. Adam was immediately posted to Iraq, others went to the Middle East and we were forgotten, left to our own devices.

Uncle Walery however had been left behind in Uzbekistan, and this was why he was able to come back for us later. He was again able to help us. Food was so scarce, we were very thin and working so hard and were so miserable, and my mother was desperate to feed her family, especially those who were having to work so hard.

One day my mother was sitting in the kibitka when she heard a chicken outside. Never one to miss an opportunity, she enticed it inside, where she somehow managed to kill it, knowing full well that if she were found out she would be severely punished by the village master for stealing scarce food. My mother didn't care. Her family were starving and she had to feed her children. It was a gift from heaven, but I sometimes wondered if it had been a dream as it seemed so bizarre! A chicken choosing to idly walk by our Kibitka!

Sometimes the children would catch a dog; they weren't brave or strong enough to kill it quickly with a hard blow to the head so instead they pushed it into a sack and suffocated it, so desperate had they become. This land had once been so abundant with pheasant, quail, wild goats and game, all now extinct.

How could Kazia get rid of the feathers? She burned them, not thinking that they would smell and cause some smoke, yet somehow she got away with it and that day we had a feast. I can't remember how she got rid of the bones, possibly she buried them too. Every time the foreman came past our kibitka we thought he was coming to punish my mother for the chicken, but somehow this didn't happen. She was very lucky.

Today my freezer is full and I am healthy and well fed, but I can never forget those days of incessant hunger. Even today, so many years after this awful experience, I tend to buy too much, tins, jars and packets of foods just in case! My children tease me about this when checking the cupboards looking for a jar of bigos or herrings and find several jars of each!

Soon after this my mother was taken ill with typhus and had to go to hospital. I had to help her, as Jasia was having to work - one of us had to work. The foreman had obtained an arba for us, pulled by mules, and we got my mother to the hospital in Vapkent. I had to leave her there and walk the five kilometres back to the collective farm . We were now alone, no mother or father, and we just prayed that she would soon recover and be back with us.

A couple of days later we were lucky enough to get some maize flour, so Jasia and I baked some buns. The next time I visited my mother in the hospital I took her some of the buns. I was only able to see her from the window as she was on an isolation ward, but though she was still very ill she recognised me. I walked back to camp with a lighter heart, knowing she was still alive. I don't remember how long she was in hospital, but she was soon better. We didn't have to cope on our own for very long. We just carried on working - we had no choice if we wanted to eat. We supported each other as Kazia would have expected us to.

The next time I went to visit her, walking the five kilometres to the hospital, alone and afraid, an Uzbek on a donkey asked me in Russian where I was going. I told him the hospital and he told me to get on the donkey. I was terrified, but I got on to the donkey. He was very insistent. After a while I said to him that I would walk the rest of the way. He agreed, but told me that he would be in the café by the bridge and to call in on the way back and I could ride back on his donkey. I was young and naïve and didn't know how to handle the situation. Was he just being kind? I didn't want to risk it.

I carried on to the hospital and took my mother some more buns. I was told by the sister on the ward when I could collect her, when she was being discharged. I didn't tell my mother about the Uzbek. When I left I ran across that bridge, hoping he wouldn't see me. I was terrified all the way back to the village, but he didn't find me. It was such a relief to see Jasia and Janusz after that particular visit to the hospital. We were all in such a heightened state of nervousness after our ordeal that we found it difficult to trust even well-meaning strangers.

After that incident we all three went to visit my mother together, and a few days later I was given a donkey to go and collect her from the hospital. She was still very weak and I don't know how she managed to sit on that donkey, but somehow we got her safely to the kibitka. We were so happy to have her back, although she would need nursing and some nourishing food, and as usual there wasn't any food to be had. The fact that she was with us somehow gave us all the strength we needed to carry on.

Soon after that Uncle Walery arrived at the collective farm from Uzbekistan. He had come to take his family and us further south so that we could be closer to the army and have a better chance of surviving and hopefully following Adam to Iraq. But it wasn't to be. Only my uncle's immediate family could be registered and allowed some food. Because Father was already posted to Iraq we were left with nothing, there was no food or money, nothing. Mammy was still recovering from her illness. She was far too ill to work, and I was in despair. How could I feed us all?

Kazia came to the rescue, she had made her mind up; she and Walery contacted a liaison officer and enrolled Jasia and me into the young cadets' school in Guzary so that we would be looked after. Janusz was too young, so she and my brother stayed behind at the Kolkhozy for now.

Ziuta and Marysia were in a collective farm further away, which was a very long walk, and we hadn't been able to see each other very often but had kept in touch. Wlodek had gone to enlist. Uncle Walery persuaded Kazia to go closer to where he was stationed so that she and Janusz would have a better chance of survival. Unless you had a family member in the army you couldn't leave the collective farm.

It was now 1942. The huge mass of Poles fleeing south was completely disorganised. Delegates from the embassy and military liaison officers were responsible for directing the movement, but the sheer vastness of the area and communication difficulties made it very demanding. To organise the many thousands leaving labour camps and prison camps was impossible and confusion was aggravated by the Ukrainians and the NKVD.

The Polish wanderers were exhausted, sick outcasts, but were uncommonly quiet and patient. We still had our determination and our resistance to hardship. Despite extreme poverty, we managed to display a certain dignity. We refused to be defeated and had great faith in God's providence. Even if you are banished to the most distant lands, the Lord God will gather you up and return you to your homeland.

Jasia and I were on our travels again to join the young cadets in Guzary, and with many other girls we travelled by arbas to Bukhara. Everything was completely disorganised, no food, no beds and we all had to sleep in the open air. It was quite frightening because there were a lot of people wandering around in the night stealing what they could, any piece of clothing, anything to barter for food. Those who haven't experienced starvation will never understand the desperation to put food in your stomach, to stop the pains. Most had bartered away everything they had in exchange for food. They had no choice left but to steal.

Somehow we got to our next stop in Guzary where the young cadets' school was gathering. The name Guzary means 'valley of death' and believe me, it was indeed the valley of death. Here nature conspired against life. It was a sandy desert, and from May the temperature could reached 103°F. The steppe would turn into a desert, with dust so thick you couldn't see through it. The water would dry up, and the local Uzbeks would leave the valley in the summer for the shade of the nearby hills. Many died there, on the threshold of freedom, from dysentery, malaria, typhus and other tropical diseases, too much for bodies which were grossly malnourished, skeletal and exhausted. Soon after I got there I contracted typhus and was very ill, and Jasia had dysentery, but neither of us succumbed. Somehow, like Mammy, we survived. We must have inherited some instinct for survival from someone, and it saw us through everything.

We were all separated at that time, Father in Iraq, Jasia and me in Guzary and my mother and Janusz in the Kolkhozy near Vapkent. At that point we didn't really think we would ever see each other again. I remember one day my fever had passed and I was allowed to go to the window to see Jasia, who had come to visit me in hospital. When she saw me she burst into tears, she was so upset. I didn't realise that I had no hair and looked like a skeleton, having lost so much weight.

Eventually I did recover to be discharged from hospital and went back to camp and soon we both recovered our strength. The Polish authorities moved us again, by train and trucks, towards Kitabu, always closer to the main point of assembly, in Pahlevi. From here we were eventually to reach Persia, or Iran as it has been renamed.

We arrived in Kitabu, after a journey of 200 kilometres from Bukhara. There was a Polish army post here, one of many scattered over southern Russia, and we were to be housed in tents, this time by a beautiful river, in a healthier climate. It was an oasis, abundant with large walnut trees, vineyards and streams, their banks covered with flowers and shrubs. The air was cooler from the mountains, but there was always danger, this time of malaria.

Neither Jasia nor I were very strong physically. I was still quite ill and I couldn't eat what they cooked because the food was very fatty and I had yellow jaundice on top of the typhus, so Jasia used to take my bread rations to the Uzbeks regardless of the fact that it wasn't allowed, and exchange it for fruit for me. She was very determined. I wasn't interested in having anything to eat. Jasia told me that I was in such a state that I only wanted to die. Our shrivelled stomachs had to become accustomed gradually to richer food, any food.

The care slowly revived me, though the effects of starvation and disease would stay with me, and many thousands of others, for some considerable time. There were lessons every day at the cadets' school, but I wasn't interested and we weren't there for very long. At least we had clean clothes and shoes on our feet. We had arrived in threadbare, filthy rags and with sore, bare feet.

I remember that one day General Anders visited our camp and told us that very soon there would be a better life for us all and we should just be patient. That gave us the hope and courage to carry on. General Anders was responsible for a powerful but exhausted tribe fleeing from Russia through the Urals and the Steppes south eastwards. They were ready to move; they were only awaiting his orders. He must have been overwhelmed at the huge demands of it all.

Soon after his visit to our camp in Kitabu we were on the move again. We were fed and prepared for another long walk to the train to Krasnowock. I was so weak I could hardly walk and couldn't carry anything, even the little we had, so Jasia had to carry all our belongings on her back. We were happy though, because we knew that at the end of our walk there would be a train waiting for us and we had each other for comfort and confidence. To have someone else to rely on and to share the tribulations of the journey was a blessing. I don't think we would have survived if we had been left to cope with this immense life change on our own. And when we arrived at the station, there it was, a lovely long passenger train, not a cattle wagon this time.

As all this was going on we didn't know what was happening to Kazia and Janusz, and we were very worried as it must have been desperate for them. In order to be able to leave with the army Janusz had to join the cadets as well, but he was too young and too short and wasn't accepted. My mother however, had other ideas and wouldn't be beaten. She put paper in his shoes to make him appear taller than he was, and he was then accepted. So my mother at long last had her remaining child a soldier in the cadets and he could travel to join the troops.

While we were on the train crawling through the mountainous part of Uzbekistan heading towards Port Krasnowock they were heading in the same direction, but at the time Jasia and I were not aware of this.

We arrived at Krasnowock, a seaport on the Caspian Sea, and spent the night there in tents. The next day, in a sandstorm so thick we couldn't see our own faces, we boarded a small ship, but not before cleaning the sand from ourselves with greasy water, which didn't help at all it just smeared the sand even further over us. We looked awful and we laughed at our futile efforts! The ship was very uncomfortable as there were very many of us and very little space, but we managed to find a small corner to lie down as I so desperately needed to lay my head somewhere. At this point I still felt so ill I didn't care if the ship sank! A lot of people on the boat were ill and there were a few deaths, mainly caused by dysentery and typhoid. People were almost dying on their feet, but they were so very determined to see it through. I remember the look in people's eyes. Some people were so traumatised they could not go on although they so desperately wanted to, while others refused to give up the fight and somehow kept going. The distances we covered were exhausting for even the fittest of us. It was some 1400 kilometresa from Kitabu to Pahlevi and the weakest had a psychological mountain to climb.

After two nights' sailing we couldn't believe our eyes at the beautiful sight that met us – an ocean. It was so very calm, and on the beach there were palm trees. At last we felt really and truly free. The nightmare of Soviet Russia and the precarious journey was over. We had made it, we were in Pahlevi in Persia, on the southern coast of the Caspian Sea, and before us there stretched a huge camp, a city of countless white tents. It was here, after the miraculous exodus from Russia, that we found our first real shelter, courtesy of the Shah of Persia. I was very weak but I had enough strength to be very happy. How had we found the energy to make that journey? We were given food, good food, and we rested and showered and were then issued with the uniforms of army cadets and allocated tents where we could lie down and rest some more.

Our first night in Pahlevi was rather stormy. No sooner had we got ready for the night than there came torrential rain and our tent, pitched on the beach, just couldn't keep the water out or hold itself up against the wind. We were absolutely soaked, but we managed to get the tent back up with some help. Then we fell back into it and slept like logs. In the morning the sun was shining and everything dried out and all was well.

Jasia and I didn't know, but Janusz was now looking for us. He had already arrived in Pahlevi, which meant that Mammy was also free. They had arrived a week before us, so Janusz was quite established there and was looking out for us as each of the loaded transports came in. Kazia must have used every ounce of her charm and persuasion on the liaison officers to get him accepted into the cadets so quickly, unless he'd grown six inches! When we saw him we couldn't believe our eyes. To have the three of us together was wonderful. We embraced each other and wept. We couldn't speak, it was too much, too emotional. We just held onto each other until we got our breath back.

Of course our next question was, 'where is Mammy?' Janusz said she was already in Teheran about 200 kilometres away with the families of the cadets who had been sent on. He had food for us, boiled eggs and some Zubrowka vodka I have never felt so much joy, you can't imagine it. And how had he got the vodka? he'd bartered for it and also for the eggs from the Persians. I forgot all about my illness and rejoiced that at last all of us were out of that desolate land, really and truly out. We were in Paradise, almost all of us together and heading towards complete freedom and a better life - just to be together would make it a better life. It had been two years since the Russians had stolen into our country and sent us to Siberia packed into cattle wagons, but my God it had felt like a lifetime, and the aching, mind-numbing terror had almost overwhelmed us.

Only those who lose their freedom can truly understand how it feels to be free again. It is so easily taken for granted and very difficult to describe how it feels to get it back. There were no guards here with rifles and dogs, and we could open and close the doors ourselves, no locks, feeling no fear. No looking over our shoulders or watching our tongues in case we said anything that might be interpreted as anti-communist! The utter joy and happiness, to smell and breathe freedom, light and air, gifts beyond imagining - it overwhelms you. Oh God, those who didn't live through it can't possibly imagine it. After two years of imprisonment and persecution in those gulags, in a land that was desolate and uninhabitable, digging into the ground and felling trees, working in snow up to our waists. We had dug through permafrost and had mostly existed on weeds and water working to the point of starvation - and the Russians came to Poland to help us! To save us from the Germans!

In Pahlevi, our training as cadets began. We were inoculated against various diseases, given rigorous disinfecting procedures, fed good food and instilled with hope. We marched up and down singing. We sang and sang, songs of joy; it was all part of our training, to let out the anguish and terror and instil confidence and morale. We knew, here and now, that Jasia and I and Janusz and Mammy were safe. Adam was also safe in Iraq, and we just prayed that the five of us would remain that way and although we were not yet all together, we soon would be. Kazia was in Teheran and all the cadets were going to move there shortly. We had heard that Walery and Zuita and their family were safely in Teheran. The grapevine that had developed was amazing. You only had to ask one person if they knew if they'd heard from Walery Radomski. If they hadn't they knew someone who probably had - the power of the spoken word and how it had travelled over such a vast land.

Within a week we were on our way, this time in big army transport wagons, with seats on both sides. The road from Pahlevi to Teheran, approximately 230 kilometres, was a treacherous mountain road. On one side of the road there were deep ravines, which was really frightening. I was sitting on the floor most of the time so I wouldn't be able to see, because I was terrified. Jasia didn't seem too bothered. She chatted to other cadets and was able to admire the beauty of the mountains and the villages in the valleys. Janusz had gone on an earlier transport with the younger men.

I remember we stopped somewhere halfway from Pahlevi to Teheran, at Tabriz. It was such a relief to stretch a little and have a drink. We stopped the night there so that the drivers could have a rest. It was still a long way to Teheran, but the road was better and I didn't have to sit on the floor this time. The journey took us through the most beautiful scenery, past vineyards, flowers and rice fields and the tree-covered slopes of the mountains of Elbrus. The scenery changed as we wound our way between high mountains and over deep ravines with less and less vegetation and then just bare rocks.

At last, we came down to Qazvin and a little later into Teheran itself and then to Camp 1. People who were already in the camp all came out of their chalets (which were built of mats of some kind) looking for relatives. And who should be there? Janusz again, with Marysia who had travelled on an earlier transport with Ziuta. But again no Kazia, where was she? Auntie Ziuta told us Mammy was in hospital, seriously ill. We were in this beautiful city of Teheran, happy at being reunited with Janusz and the others with the worst behind us, and we had this terrible news about Mammy. Starvation had left a terrible mark on us all, but on top of her heart condition it had almost killed her.

We were in a completely different world. Teheran was a city full of hustle and bustle, the shops were full of goods and the people were very kind. The Persians carried baskets on their heads and sold all manner of goods, dried fruits, cigarettes, boiled eggs and so on. Nobody had any money, so people exchanged whatever they could to buy something. At this stage they had next to nothing, having bartered away most of their possessions. We were welcomed by a people who were extremely kind and respectful of our situation and who were also very generous towards us, especially with their time. They couldn't do enough. We were so indebted to them.

Two years of living with the deprivation imposed by the Russians had not prepared us for the overwhelming sight of shops full of goods and cleanliness. We were able to bathe and enjoy the fresh sea air and eventually enjoy the good food. To us wearied Poles, nothing more than skin and bone, a plentiful supply of fresh fruits helped with our physical recovery

Ala and Jasia, Caspian Sea,
Pahlevi, c 1942

Ala and Jasia, Teheran
Hospital, c 1942

SANCTUARY ON THE CASPIAN SEA

It was the autumn of 1942 when we were settling into Camp 1 in Teheran, and we still hadn't had any news about Adam. Oh how desperately we needed him. We found out later through Antoni, who had worked so hard for all of us, that all this time he was looking for us through the Red Cross.

The day after we arrived in Teheran, Jasia and I went to the hospital to see Mammy. She was very ill, but so happy to see us and relieved to know we were safe. Hospitals had opened in Pahlevi and Isfahan with the assistance of the Red Cross and the Polish-American Relief Organisation. Five refugee camps opened in Meshed and Achwaz, hostels for the elderly and an orphanage and community centre. Yes we were all safe, but so ill. Exhaustion and the sudden change in living conditions caused diseases to break out, primarily dysentery and typhoid, and many people died, so close to freedom. Grief touched thousands of people. It was hard to accept. People we knew were dying around us; one day they seemed to be recovering and the next they had died. Perhaps the calm after so intense a mental pressure and physical hardship had been just too much to bear and the body was too weak and gave out. So very sad, it affected us all. Many hundreds of bodies lie in the Dulab cemetery in south Tehran having almost touched freedom

Soon we had to choose what to do. Jasia decided that because I was still so sick after having typhus and yellow jaundice, I should remain in Teheran and stay with Kazia and Janusz. The rest of the cadets were being sent to Palestine, as were the more able-bodied men and women of military age to prepare for active service. So with Jasia gone, Kazia, Janusz and I stayed in Teheran waiting for news of Adam. Ziuta and Marysia also stayed with us, both recovering from typhus and dysentery, before Marysia could also join the cadets in Palestine.

My father had now found out where we were, and in 1943 he came to see us on leave from Iraq. It was a lovely and very emotional reunion. He was able to stay for two weeks, and it was wonderful to have him there. The relief at being free was overwhelming, sometimes I couldn't breathe. We were all having difficulty getting used to these new circumstances. There were no guards with barking dogs but we were still edgy, expecting shouted orders from intimidating guards. It would take some time to adjust. We knew we were free, but it was difficult to believe that freedom was really here to stay once the gulag had been a part of our lives.

In January 1943, the Soviet Government sent a note

to the Polish Government in London informing them that all Poles remaining in Russia who had originated from the provinces under Russian occupation, including the eastern Borderlands, would be considered Soviet subjects. The Russian authorities offered no assistance whatsoever and those Poles who were incapable of making that most arduous journey to freedom, through age, exhaustion, infirmity or lack of dependents, were condemned to endless captivity away from their homeland. With no help from the Soviets, they would have died if they had undertaken that formidable journey. In Kazakhstan alone, 120,000 people can trace their Polish origins, and there many survivors remain, often in abject poverty.

Very slowly, day, by day, Kazia was getting better, and at last the day arrived of her discharge from hospital. I remember the day I went to collect her we were so happy being together again.

Ala 3rd from right, back row, Teheran c 1943

Kazia, Ala, Janusz, Adam, c 1943   *Kazia, c 1943*

The three of us, Kazia, Janusz and I, were in Camp 1 for now, but for how long we didn't know, because the authorities were moving people all the time. There wasn't enough space for us all in Teheran. Some had to go to Africa and some to India, while a lot of orphaned children were sent to Isfahan, where schools were organised for them. These young children were in such a state of shock, almost a comatose state. Some had siblings to help them bear the awful situation but some were totally alone in the world. How would they cope with this at such a young age?

Wherever our people were sent, schools were immediately organised so that they wouldn't miss too much schooling. The children hadn't had any schooling to speak of whilst they had been in the Russian labour camps for the past two years, except for having to learn Russian and the communistic ways of their Russian masters. Their parents did their best to make sure this didn't happen. They were determined the children should remain Poles, and they succeeded

Mammy and I were getting quite fit after our illness in Uzbekistan and I had put on a little weight and was beginning to feel better. I got a job in the camps, sewing with my Auntie Ziuta, which was wonderful because I was earning some money and Mammy and I could go to the shops and buy some material and make clothes.

At long last we heard from Adam, who was still very ill with typhus in Iraq. We had a letter from him and a photograph of him with Jasia. They had met in Iraq, Jasia and the rest of the cadets having stopped there on the way to Palestine. Completely by chance, they had found each other in the camps. We always seemed to be able to find each other when many others only faced disappointment.

Strange and wonderful things did happen whilst the Poles were evacuating Russian labour camps. On one of the trains from Swierdlowsk near the Ural mountains, we noticed a young boy approach one of the men waiting to get into the wagon. He said "Daddy, is it you?" The man didn't pay any attention, lost in thought, but the boy persisted, and the man then looked at the boy and recognised him and burst into tears. They hugged and the boy told him that his mother and sisters were further down the line. Very few families survived as a unit, and this was one very lucky family, as we were.

So by autumn 1943 we had all been found. Although not yet all together, we all knew where each other was - it was a miracle. But now we were on the move again. The authorities were sending people to Africa, India and other places. My mother didn't want to go to Africa so we chose Isfahan.

We collected our meagre belongings and were ready for another journey. The buses were quite comfortable after the trucks we'd travelled in from Pahlevi to Teheran and the roads were in better condition along the edge of the Great Salt Desert. It was very dry, we didn't see any vegetation, trees or people for many miles and the villages were very few. It was just desert for most of the 280 kilometres journey and enduring the climate was very difficult.

The journey lasted many hours and we were desperate for food and water. We had stopped along the route at various shelters, hamlets and shacks. We found shelter to rest for a while, but no food and very little water. Only occasionally did we see an oasis with water.

When the buses rolled into Isfahan we were taken aback at the beautiful surroundings. Trees and flowers bursting with such vivid colours. Homes were surrounded by very large gardens. We spent the night in the courtyard of a large building which we learned later was the palace of the Armenian Bishop.

Next day we were allocated living quarters and settled in. Auntie Ziuta got a job in one of the schools as a carer and I got a job in a hospital, in charge of the stores. I wasn't in this post for long because as I had been in the Girl Guides in Poland my superiors offered me a job as a secretary of all the Scouts and Girl Guides in Isfahan.

They actually made me accept the job, probably because there wasn't anyone else who was yet fit enough! Of course it was a much better job. As well as a secretary I was also a Cub leader. I thoroughly enjoyed the job. My Cubs were called Krechowiecy, after Adam and Walery's cavalry regiment.

Ala, second right, 1943

Ala, right, with fellow Scout leaders, Camp 3 1943

Adam, Wlodek (Walery's elder son) and Walery, 1943

Life was very pleasant in Isfahan, the old capital of
Persia, as we knew it then. It had once been a major
empire with settlements dating back to 4000 BC. A
monarchy ruled by a Shah from 1501 until the 1979
Iranian revolution when Iran became an Islamic republic.

It was now 1944 and I was enjoying my job and
making friends. Janusz was happy at cadet school, but my
mother once again was not very well. She was suffering
because the climate of Isfahan didn't agree with her heart
condition and all the other ailments she had succumbed
to along the way. She had difficulties breathing and the
stress on her heart was beginning to tell, maybe because
of the height above sea level.

We stayed there until my father was discharged from
the army. He had developed a stomach ulcer and hadn't
fully recovered from the debilitating typhus. He wasn't

considered fit enough for duty and in the end he was discharged from the army as being unfit for service. He was hugely disappointed and was never easy about his inability to join the troops. He also, like his fellow deportees, had been able to control his feelings towards his new ally, Russia. He had somehow contained the hatred he felt towards Russia for invading his country, transporting many thousands of his countrymen to unheard-of destinations and trying to crush the Polish spirit. In this last case, they had been unsuccessful! Instead, taking the lead from General Anders, all had sworn loyalty to their former captors and like him only wanted to fight the Germans.

In Isfahan we had an Anglo-Polish club which was frequented by the British airmen who were stationed there. We had been well fed and clothed by the British Army and were beginning to relax and ready to enjoy some

Wlodek Radomski, Tehran 1943

Zbyszek Radomski

Jasia, Nazareth, 1944

Ala, Kazia, Tehran 1943

Janusz, Kazia, Adam, Ala, 1944

Janusz, 1944

Ala, Adam, Kazia and Janusz, 1943

socialising. Film shows were held there, and concerts and meetings. One evening at a film show there was a young airman who asked our librarian to introduce him to me. His name was Taffy. He started talking to me and telling me where he lived in Britain. He took me home that evening, although I wasn't very impressed by him.

One afternoon my friend Irena and I were in the club and there were two airmen there. Irena introduced me to them; one was called Harry and the other Bill. After that initial encounter we met occasionally when Harry and Bill were off duty and would have a game of cards. They were wireless operators and their job was to send weather reports to the Forces. They also helped us to learn English and we continued to socialise with them.

Soon it was Christmas 1944 and we had a very quiet, and reflective one. Our thoughts were of home and Wigilia, which we celebrate on Christmas eve. It is the most important culinary event of the year. At one time dinner consisted of 12 courses, representing the 12 Apostles, but today it is far more modest. Even to think about those 12 courses was too much for our recovering appetites, but our mouths watered thinking about the Uszka (little ears) with the barszcz (beetroot soup), fried carp with mushrooms and sauerkraut, golabki (cabbage parcels) pierogi, soused herrings and of course the poppy seed roll and cheese cake. It was something else to focus our minds on and look forward to in the future.

In Isfahan there was an English mission run by a lady called Mrs Mentle, and she had organised a party for the English airmen with their guests for Twelfth Night. We all met at my friend Irena's flat. By now Taffy had assumed that I was his girlfriend and that he was taking me to the party, which was a surprise to me, but I went along with it as it had been prearranged.

We all arrived at Mrs Mentle's and it was very nice. There was a gramophone; lovely records playing and couples were dancing. I was itching to dance because I loved dancing, and still do. Taffy just sat there, hardly speaking to me and not asking me to dance. I later learned that he couldn't dance. Bill took pity on me. He got Taffy to another room and tried to teach him a few steps of tango, but of course he was useless. So in the end Bill asked me to dance and we danced for the rest of the evening. I'm not sure where a Lancashire mill lad had learned to tango! But I was pleased, we had fun and I was beginning to relax. Bill was also more talkative and easier to get on with.

Once the dancing was over and it was time to leave, we all started the walk home. Taffy tagged along with us, still thinking I was his girlfriend, yet making no effort to talk to me! I was now confused, obviously out of step with the mind of a Welshman! Bill was walking behind us and I thought, I'm not walking with this dummy, so I called to ask Bill if he was going the same way and stepped back in line with him.

We walked together the rest of the way. The night was so beautiful, a full moon was shining and it was starting to snow lightly, and I'd shaken Taffy off. Bill walked me home and then went on to his station.

After that evening Taffy didn't have a good word to say about me (I heard this from Bill) and never spoke to me again. Should I have been pleased? Bill wasn't too happy about Taffy's attitude as I'd not done anything wrong but had been completely misinterpreted. However, Bill and I then became friendly, and met several times at Mrs Mentle's. Soon after that he was posted again to Teheran.

Ala and Kazia, Isfahan, 1944

Ala, Janusz and Kazia, Isfahan

The Scout Group, Isfahan, Ala back left; I was one of the leaders and thoroughly enjoyed my time organising events with the scouts Isfahan, 1944

Ala, Janusz, Ziuta, Kazia, Marysia, Isfahan

Bill and friend, Isfahan

Ala and Bill, Isfahann

Isfahan, 1944

In the meantime Adam was notified that he had to go back to Teheran to join his army unit, and Janusz and Kazia were to go there with him, to a bigger camp, Camp 3, which was much better equipped to deal with the many people needing medical assistance. It was a place with many green trees and bushes and a little stream, and this would better suit my mother's health and she would be nearer to medical aid.

I was still at my post as a secretary in Isfahan when we heard that there was going to be a nursing course there. My auntie Ziuta thought we ought to enrol, which we did. The course was to be held at the Polish Red Cross HQ in Teheran, so back to Teheran we all went, and I hoped that Bill would find me. I liked him, he was good company and very loving and attentive.

The lessons started and I was quite enjoying school again. We were informed that when we passed the exams we would be posted to the Middle East, Egypt, Palestine or Italy. My mother wouldn't hear of it as we had been separated already, and she couldn't bear another parting, so she persuaded me to take a job as a typist in the camp where she was living. She had already spoken to the Camp Commandant about me and hoped he would be helpful.

I had passed the typing course previously when we were in Camp 1 before we went to Isfahan. I went to the Camp Commandant, introduced myself and got the job on the spot. All I had to do was to type a letter of application. I was quite happy to be a typist in Camp 3 if it meant staying close to Mammy, and not putting any unnecessary burden on her.

While I was on the nurses' course Bill had been looking for me in Isfahan, and as I hadn't let him know where I had moved to he had to look for me again. He always found me wherever I was - he was very determined. He was the same as Uncle Walery, who despite sometimes overwhelming odds always found his way back to the family.

In the meantime my father, who had just rejoined his unit in Teheran, had to go to Egypt to be formally discharged. All this was taking time and we knew we would all be leaving Teheran soon - we all had to leave Persia. We were being moved all the time but we never knew when. We had to make room for other deportees who were arriving all the time. In the meantime we were all working. My mother had a little job sewing, I was typing and Janusz went to lessons. We had a dog called Ass and we were living in tents, but we knew we would soon be on the move again. Events moved quickly; we were never given much warning, just enough time to pack.

In late 1945 we learned of our next destination. From Teheran we had to pack and move all the way to Beirut in the Lebanon, a journey of around 1600 kilometres. First we had to go by train from Teheran to Arak, staying overnight, then by army lorries to a camp in Baghdad. We stayed only for a few days as the intention was to move us on to our next destination without too much delay.

Before we were moved from Teheran, Bill had to leave for Iraq, and before he left he asked me to marry him. He must already have asked me half a dozen times, and each time I said no. At that time I had seven 'boyfriends', just friends I had met in the different camps on our travels, all in the forces in Palestine, Egypt and Iraq. They were all writing letters to me, and they were all Poles. You can imagine my predicament. I was seeing Bill, an Englishman, so very loving, declaring his love for me, and refusing to take no for an answer. But each time I said no, because I just didn't want to leave Mammy. After so many separations and such hardships it would be so difficult. I was still so young and adapting to a very different life and trying to absorb all that had happened to us.

A watercolour by Wm. Hartley (Bill) c 1945 – Demavent, the site of my marriage proposal. Bill did several water colours of our time together in the Middle East. He was also a talented calligrapher and in later life ran his own printing business.

The next time Bill asked me to marry him, we were having a day out in the mountains at Demavent, where the Shah of Persia had his summer residence. It was Bill's last day in Teheran and it was lovely. We had our favourite place to sit, a tree stump by a little stream. It was very calm there and so peaceful, listening to the river slowly running by and watching the sun and the shadows shimmer on the water. It was so romantic and I'm not ashamed to say that I am a romantic at heart! It was an ideal place for a proposal.

As we sat there, Bill was talking of his love for me, asking me to marry him again because he knew he would have to leave Teheran with the RAF very soon. He didn't know when or where he would be posted.

I slowly stopped writing to my other boyfriends and continued seeing Bill, and on his last day of leave in Teheran, I finally said yes, I would marry him, he loved me so much. But was I doing the right thing?

Bill and Ala, Tehran, 1944/5   *Ala & Jasia, Ghazir, 1945*

Bill and Ala, Tehran, 1946

Ala, Tehran, 1944/5

Ala, Tehran, 1944/5

Ala and Jasia, Ghazir, 1945

Ala, Bill and Alexandria, Tehran, 1944/5

I had always intended to say yes, but there was so much else to think of and I couldn't agree to marriage so easily. There was my family, and their future was still so unsettled. We had been reunited for such a short time.

Bill left Teheran a much happier man though, as he headed off with all the other airmen for Habbaniyah in Iraq. I missed him after he left, but he wrote every day. As soon as he got to his camp, Habbaniyah, he applied immediately to the RAF authorities for permission to marry me. He hadn't wasted any time! The Lancashire lad who could tango had claimed his girl and wanted to make her officially his without delay!

It was going to take a long time for the formalities and in the meantime we were getting on with life and preparing for more travels. We had now arrived in Baghdad and were to travel on by train from there, moving towards the Lebanon and crossing the Turkey-Syria border to reach Aleppo in Syria. It wasn't very safe for us to be transported at that time because there was much unrest in those countries, but we eventually got through the borders after some delay sorting out the papers and permission to cross.

Aleppo was the second city of Syria, today the scene of civil unrest between President Assad and rebel forces . There have been many previous conflicts with the Syrians, against the Persians, Greeks and Romans until Arab Islamic conquest in 636 AD. Since the 3rd millennium BC Syria was a flourishing city, a meeting point of many commercial routes in the north. A centre of trade with France, Turkey, England and Holland, it now lies mostly in ruins, bombarded by heavy weaponry, the ancient mosque and minaret devastated by artillery.

In Aleppo there were some British soldiers waiting for us with hot drinks, for which we were extremely grateful as we hadn't had anything to drink for 24 hours. There were also Polish soldiers in British uniforms looking happy and confident, and it was so reassuring to see them. They had waited for us, despite the delays, until the middle of the night. In Aleppo we had to transfer from the passenger train to the goods train for some reason, and this was to be the last part of our journey for some time. We spent a nervous night in Aleppo, very much aware of the unrest but knowing there were British soldiers on hand to protect us.

From Aleppo all our people were allocated different places to go, which meant separations from newly-made friends. My mother, Janusz and I were to go to a house in a village on the top of a mountain. It was beautiful, right by the Mediterranean, in a village called Ghazir, just outside Beirut. It was lovely, but my mother couldn't make the walk down the mountain, her health was still so precarious.

It was nearly Christmas 1945 and my father was officially demobbed and was coming to join us. Jasia was coming for Christmas and Bill was coming too, as he still had to officially ask my father for my hand in marriage.

When Bill and I were apart waiting for official permission to be married he wrote me countless letters, sometimes two a day, and I still have them. It was going to be a very memorable Christmas, as it was our first

Christmas together as a family for three years. It was quiet though, as we were still unsettled and unsure of our future. After Christmas Bill had to go back to Iraq and Jasia back to Palestine, where she was at teacher training college and still a cadet, but for the moment it was a happy time.

MARRIAGE IN LEBANON

Lebanon was a beautiful country. The name means white, a reference to the snow-capped Mount Lebanon. It took my breath away. We were able to walk down the Serpentine to the sea; coming back up the steep incline with the cedars in the background, was rather exhausting but we enjoyed it.

Bill had got permission from my father to marry me, so it was now a matter of waiting for permission from the RAF and also from the Archbishop of the Catholic Church to be married in a Catholic church. This was necessary because Bill wasn't a Catholic at that time. So we had to wait for the authorisations.

It wasn't until many years later that I realised the historical importance of the countries we had journeyed through. My concentration then was purely on getting through one day at a time! Whilst I had appreciated the beauty and the wonder I had not been aware of their significance. We had set foot on some of the oldest continuously-inhabited cities in the world, dating back to earlier than 5000 BC .

Bill was still writing two or even three letters every day, but I wasn't a very good letter writer, so I didn't write to him very often. Soon after Christmas in 1945 my father asked permission from the authorities to move us from the house on the mountain down the Serpentine because my mother couldn't possibly walk all the way to the shops and church. In the meantime I was the shopper, the little donkey bringing the shopping home.

Within a short time we were offered a place with an Arab family down the Serpentine, and my mother was happy because she was able to walk to the shops and church. Her heart condition was so bad and she had difficulty breathing, which is why she couldn't walk any great distance, especially uphill. That Kazia had survived so far was a wonder. She had incredible strength of mind and will.

It was now 1946 and we were looking forward to planning the wedding. Bill's parents were in England, so they were not able to come; it would have been impossible for them to travel. Eventually, Bill got the permission from the RAF to be married and we also had approval from the Archbishop to be married in a Catholic church. This all took about six months, but the time flew by.

Now it was time to arrange the date. Our Polish parish priest was to marry us on the 9th July. My mother and I went to Beirut to get some material for my wedding dress. It was very lovely heavy crepe, which the tailor was to make into a most beautiful gown.

Unfortunately Bill's parents weren't happy about him marrying someone from another religion who was also a foreigner, and they would not give their blessing to the marriage. My mother and my father, although they liked Bill, weren't sure about him either, feeling they hadn't known him long enough. They also weren't happy about the 'mixed' marriage, and the fact that I was going to move so far away, especially after the family had only just been reunited. Their futures were also so uncertain. The Poles in the Middle East had been given the choice of England, America, and Africa to go to, or back to Poland. We had nothing to go back to, like many other families who had lost everything, and my father feared that he would be arrested again by the Soviets having fought in the 1920 uprising against them - and the Russians never forget, their record-keeping and memory are meticulous.

We found out years later, that former deportees, especially from the eastern borderlands, were treated extremely harshly by the Soviet dictatorship in post-war Poland, many being imprisoned on trumped-up charges, others sent to gulags, some just disappearing, and some were executed

Signals XI, Habbaniyah 1943, Bill 2nd left back row

Signals XI, Sharjah, Bill 1st left back row

The family together for Christmas, Ghazir 13.12.1945

My parents, although uncertain about it, gave their blessing to our wedding. I was busy learning English and Bill was trying his best with learning Polish, but communication was still a little difficult. Despite all reservations, the wedding was set for the 9th July at 6 pm. I must confess to a feeling of bewilderment. I seemed to be seeing everything through a very thick fog it just didn't seem real.

Jasia and my cousin Marysia, also a cadet, were coming from Palestine. Everything was going well, but as the date approached our priest informed us that the wedding would have to be on July 10th instead. I don't remember the reason why, but it must have been something important. Our wedding rings had been engraved for the 9th, so they had to stay like that.

Two days before the wedding Bill and his best man Eric arrived from Habbaniya in Iraq and Jasia and Marysia arrived the same day from Palestine. Two of my best friends were present, Nusia and Irena. Walery and Wlodek were in Iraq with the British forces and Ziuta was with them, so they weren't able to get leave to be with us. The day of the wedding was lovely, hot and sunny. We sat under the lemon trees and grapevines on the terraces at the house where we had rented a room. The landlord and his family also lived there with two other families. We were being supported by money from the Polish authorities to cover our living needs.

It wasn't a big wedding, as it might have been at home in Poland, where it would have been a huge event. We didn't have much, having lost everything, our osada in the country and our apartment, the Russians taking all our land and possessions before we'd even boarded the cattle wagons towards exile. The friends and families of the NKVD had not wasted time moving in. But we were free, and it was such a lovely day. There were about 20 of us. My friend Irena, who was my maid of honour, dressed me to be ready to be at the church for 6 pm. When Bill came to the house, he was quite nervous; it was so different for him, coming into a foreign family and their customs, although he liked my family very much. Yet I was quite calm.

It was only a short walk to the church, and it was a beautiful evening in Ghazir. Bill and I walked slowly up the hill towards the church. I was carrying flowers, still holding onto that calmness. I was only 22 whilst Bill, who was 26, was stricken with nerves. We chatted, and then entered the church. I thought there would only be my friends there; I really didn't want a big wedding so I hadn't told many people, but I was quite well known and liked by my people within the Polish community and was in the church choir, so word had got round and everyone seemed to know about my wedding.

The church was full, mostly with Poles from all the different camps on our travels, friends from Persia, army personnel etc. There were also some Arabs from the village who had heard that a Polish girl was getting married and were curious about a European wedding. It was a wonderful surprise, and I was so happy. Bill was still very nervous, yet surprisingly I was still quite calm.

So we were married in a French church, by a Polish priest, in a mostly Arab village called Ghazir, not far from Beirut. When we came out of the church Janusz took photographs. It was still early evening and warm and we had a taxi home this time. We could have walked the short distance, but my mother and father spoiled us, so we had a ride.

My parents were home before us and met us at the door with bread and salt, as is the Polish custom, to welcome the newly-married couple home. The guests arrived soon afterwards and we had a drink, probably a very generous shot of vodka if Janusz was pouring and some wine. It wasn't a lavish wedding, but supper was delicious. in later years at each special occasion or get-together, we always called Janusz's shots of vodka, a 'Polish measure'. Janusz had a very good arm! This talent seems to run in the family.

With the help of Jasia we've been able to remember a few details of the wedding supper. I also recall that Mammy cooked everything on two primus stoves, very primitive, but there was nothing else. We had very little to our name, but we had a very safe haven as displaced people, and of course we had each other and we held on very tight.

How Mammy was able to prepare such a wonderful feast I'll never know but she had always been so resourceful. There was barszcz (beetroot soup), mushroom pierogi, (meat parcels), herrings with apples, beetroot salad, fried chicken, dumplings, golabki (meat parcels in cabbage) meatloaf with stuffed eggs and rice, meatballs and rice, mizeria (cucumber salad & soured cream) gherkins, olives, pitta bread, pancakes and oranges, dates and grapes.

She must have sold her soul, what a banquet! And what a wonderful recovered memory. It took a few phone calls with my sister but we got there in the end. We would have had something very similar back home in Poland.

Our wedding photographs show us all in a very serious mood. Although it was a happy occasion, under the surface we were still feeling the effects of our experiences in Russia, and would suffer flashbacks for many years to come. Everyone also knew that we were to be separated yet again as I was going to England with Bill, and this was heavy on our minds.

Wedding day – 10th July 1946, Ghazir

The wedding group – Janusz, Marysia, Adam, Ala, Bill,
Jasia, Kazia, Eric, Irena and friend

Later in the evening when our guests had left, Bill and I danced on the terrace under the vines and stars, to some lovely music, mostly tango. It was a reflective, quiet moment, but there was a slight problem - we had no bed for the night. Our Arab landlord had double-booked the room we were to have, and there was only one other room for the whole family. We didn't find out about the double booking until later in the evening, so it was impossible to make other arrangements. That night Bill slept on the roof garden and I slept downstairs with my sister. So our wedding night was a little different, but still memorable! We were happy, and it didn't really matter as it was such a minor thing in the circumstances.

After that we did make other arrangements. It was only for a few nights after all. Then Bill was taken ill with papadach, a tropical disease with very high fever, and then he was due to go back to Habbaniyah. So only a week after our wedding we were to be separated. With Bill and Eric back on duty I was left without a husband. I was however with Mammy, Daddy and Janusz.

Soon after that we moved house again, nearer the centre of Ghazir, closer still for Mammy to get to the shops and church. We lived, shopped and saw friends. Jasia and Marysia were in Palestine as we waited for the family's future to be decided. Bill continued writing wonderful letters, and that kept me going. He had to wait for all formalities from the RAF to be completed in preparation for taking me to England as his wife, and we had to cover quite a lot of officialdom and ground before that happened. I was feeling very guilty, sad and apprehensive about leaving my family and also very anxious about what to expect in England, meeting Bill's family, it was almost too much.

At last in October, Bill came to collect me. He stayed overnight and the following day we had to leave for Cairo. I packed my suitcase and had to say goodbye to my family. It was very, very hard because I didn't know if I would ever see them again. We all cried. It was heartbreaking and my parents were distraught.

Kazia and Adam did eventually decide to go to England, as Jasia was to travel there to share lodgings with a friend outside London, finishing her teacher training course, so the decision was an easy one to make. There was nothing in Poland to go back to. All of the Osada Krechowiecka and surrounding lands and forests had been razed to the ground, torched, leaving nothing, no surface, no history, just emptiness. Who would want to make claim to that? It was Stalin's! He had regained land previously lost in some long-ago battle and he'd spoiled it because it was his and because he could! A purely malevolent act by a petulant tyrant. It was such a naturally, beautiful forested land, yet no one else could ever farm, inhabit or enjoy it. Madness!

Bill and I travelled from Ghazir by taxi to Beirut and from there took another taxi to Haifa (Lebanon to Palestine). We stayed overnight at Haifa, in the YMCA. Next day we took a taxi and train to Jerusalem, where we stayed two days and were able to see something of the city. We didn't see very much because of the rebellion. There was terrible unrest at the time and we were not able to move around freely, and Bill had to report to camp. We left Jerusalem heading for Cairo by train, which was a very long journey.

Although we were very newly wed, our start to married life wasn't very romantic. The journeys were very long and uncomfortable over 250 kilometres so far and it was all very tiring, with trouble spots along the way. I was also so sad missing my parents, knowing they were inconsolable after losing me so soon after our reunion following the hardship of the labour camps.

After a journey to Cairo of 280 kilometres we took a

taxi to our hotel, the Hermitage House, and at last we could rest on a comfortable bed. After our rest we took a shower and went down to the dining room to have something to eat. It was heaven, lovely food, and it was the first time we had eaten fresh dates from the tree. We spent six lovely weeks in Cairo at the expense of the RAF, waiting for a boat to take us to England because I wouldn't fly, I was still in such an anxious state.

It was very hot during the day, so we went out in the evenings to open-air cinemas or to the Gropis café in Cairo, where we danced among the palm trees in the gardens, getting back to the hotel in the early hours of the morning. We couldn't go out freely because of the tensions in the Middle East at that time, and we had to be very cautious. It was quite frightening as troops were on the streets in large numbers, on high alert, and you could feel the anxiety in the ordinary people on the streets.

Tensions had escalated after the bombing in July of the King David Hotel, which was the administrative HQ for the British forces in Palestine. The Irgun, a militant Zionist movement were responsible.

This had been in response to a raid on the Jewish Agency by the British authorities, on Black Sabbath. The British had confiscated incriminating information about the Jewish Agency's involvement with violent acts and this information had been taken to the King David Hotel. The Irgun were determined to destroy this information and planted explosives in milk churns in the basement. To avoid suspicion they had dressed mostly as Arabs and the guards were easily overcome. The explosion caused the collapse of the southern wing of the hotel, causing many deaths and injuries to those who were in the road outside.

Despite this state of unrest we made the most of our extended honeymoon. Our married life began with a mixture of conflicting memories and yet more unrest, but we knew life could only get easier from here and were looking forward to married life.

Bill, Habbaniyah, 1945

Ala, Teheran, 1945

CHAPTER EIGHT

THOUGHTS OF A SURVIVOR

Jan Wojcik, a well known journalist and the 'Voice of Solidarnosc', during his last broadcast on Radio, said: "I was forced to leave half a century ago and it is where I left that most essential part of my being – my heart. Poland is inside me". After 50 years of wandering he went back to his birthplace, Volhynia.

"There had been a delightfully developed osada in which had stood my home, surrounded by a garden and fertile fields" he wrote. "Nothing, but nothing, remained of any of this. Everything had been razed to the ground. Even trees and forests had been put to the torch so that no one could ever recognise his roots, and wouldn't dare put a claim to it."

They craved the very roots,
Desired the furrows groove swallow the top soil deep
So that nothing, no surface remained;
No linking with the last –
No past – no history

Of her and of this nation
Whose prediluvian line was nurtured here
Through countless generations.
They sought to smooth over the marks,
The tiniest traces of dust.
Disfigured, drove, dispelled,
Divided the heart from the head.
But one granule they quite overlooked
The grit of the Land itself

- Feliks Konarsk

My cousin, Marek Skocyzlas, son of my cousin Marysia, made a claim in his Grandfather Walery's name for the return of the lands of his Osada, but was unsuccessful.

In 1988, after a wave of strikes, the Communist Party in Poland agreed to share political power. On April 5th 1989 an agreement was signed in which the party and representatives from the Solidarnosc movement specified their conditions. In the elections of 1989 Solidarnosc thrashed the communists, winning almost every seat it contested. Lech Walesa, Solidarnosc's leader, was elected president of Poland in 1990. The election of Cardinal Karol Wojtyla as Pope had strengthened the people's resolve in coping with the realities of communism, and on one of his early visits to his homeland he had encouraged millions of his countrymen with the words "do not be afraid". He returned to Poland in 1991 to enjoy with his people a free Poland. Full sovereignty was regained in

1992 with the withdrawal of most of the Soviet occupying troops. Poland then returned, officially, to Christianity. The Poles ever resourceful, had followed their faith throughout, although quietly. The Soviets couldn't really arrest an entire country, despite their domination!

The events in Poland, the first country in the eastern bloc to throw off the shackles of communist tyranny, inspired the collapse of communism in Europe as a whole. Adapting to a free society and economy has not been as smooth as some Poles might have hoped, but the country has emerged from the mire and is now a member of the European Union. How I wish my parents had lived long enough to see their homeland free again. They at least lived out their days in the freedom of England.

The London victory celebrations of 1946 were British Commonwealth, Empire and Allied victory celebrations held after the defeat of Nazi Germany and Japan. These celebrations took place in London on 8th June 1946, consisting of a military parade through the city and a night-time fireworks display. Most Allied countries took part in this parade, but Poland was deliberately excluded and our country's lack of representation caused huge controversy.

This was because the British Labour Government had caved in to Stalin's demands with a whimper. Stalin did not want the Poles included in the celebrations and the Labour government did not want to anger the new Stalin-approved communist government in Poland. Polish fighters, eastern borderlands deportees, in fact, anyone

Polish who had fought so valiantly with the other Allies were therefore left out because the British Government was more concerned with post-war relations with Stalin than celebrating and acknowledging their ally Poland's war efforts. In later years it was claimed that the Soviets' reach extended to the militants of the unions in their determination to cause massive disruption to the British economy during the strikes of the 1970s and 1980s.

The Poles who were so instrumental to the Allied war effort, having played key roles in the Battle of Britain, Squadron 303 was made up of fearless, some would say reckless, Polish airmen who with air cadets had made their way to England across war-torn Europe to enlist and fight the Germans. They have only recently been acknowledged as the foremost squadron in the RAF during the Battle of Britain, with the most kills. The conflicts at Monte Cassino, Falaise Gap, Normandy and the Warsaw Uprising, were forgotten. Those brave Polish servicemen were not invited to participate in the Victory Parade, because of pressure from Stalin on the Labour Government. It was a final betrayal, a callous act of political duplicity. This was one of the most shameful acts of the Cold War and a spineless labour Government.

Jasia's feelings on this were explosive, right up to her last days in 2011. The anger never left her.

Hugh Dalton, a former Chancellor of the Exchequer, said in 1940 "On the day of victory, Poland, as the first nation to stand up to Hitler whilst others grovelled to him, should ride in the van of the victory march". Winston

Churchill added "Her Majesty's Government will never forget the debt they owe to the Polish troops who have served them so valiantly and for those who have fought under our command". It was only recently (2002) that the son of a Polish veteran, Michael Moszynski, moved by the injustice of it all, secured an official apology from appropriately, a British Labour PM.

We Poles in our thousands had watched from the streets in tears. This hurtful insult persists to this day, despite the apology, 60 years too late. For us it was a question of honour.

On the 15th August 1992, The Poles, ignoring the platitudes of the politically-correct English elite, decided to have their own victory parade in Warsaw, the first parade since the end of the war. The Polish war veterans, deportees and relatives of deportees, walked with pride and honour through the streets of Warsaw.

As Wieslaw Wolwowicz of the Polish 2nd Corps put it: "We were the allies, the allies of the British, and we weren't even invited to take part in the victory parade after the war. We were like people who'd done the hard work and whom nobody wanted any more".

It would seem the Poles were being looked upon as "non-persons" again, which is how the Soviets looked upon the deportee Poles! The Remembrance Sunday parade in London has only recently begun inviting Polish survivors of Russia's ethnic cleansing of the eastern borderlands and other areas to participate. The numbers are few, and efforts must be made to encourage more survivors and children of survivors to attend.

Many of the stories of the people from the Borderlands who were exiled to the wastes of Russia remain untold. Stalin deported almost two million Poles to Siberia and other outreaches of Russia. No politicians honour the victims in speeches commemorating WWII. Accounts of the war are incomplete without acknowledging this historical tragedy. The gap is slowly being filled, not by Governments or associations for memorials but by ordinary people, survivors and relatives of survivors. The account deserves official recognition.

A NEW HOME IN ENGLAND

At the beginning of November 1946 we were to board the ship *Durban Castle* bound for England. It was a passenger ship converted into an army carrier. We left Cairo by train for Port Said, a journey of over 2000 kilometres travelling alongside the Suez Canal. When we arrived in Port Said in the early evening I saw a very big ship anchored some way from the shore, and while we were waiting for our papers to be checked, I wondered how we were going to reach it. It was such a long way out and I was beginning to feel very nervous.

It was already dark when we were to board the ship and we had to walk on pontoons all the way to it. The pontoons were moving and it all looked quite scary. We lined up in our hundreds, all very wary, mostly very young women, brides of English servicemen.

We started to walk towards the pontoons, one foot in front of the other, not daring to look between the gaps. When we got to the end of the pontoons we had to climb up some steps, and seeing the water between the stairs was really frightening. All this happened in the dark, although the ship was lit up and gave us a bit of light to see where we were putting our feet. The ship was moving all the time, even while we were boarding. I was very relieved to eventually board.

There were hundreds of people on board. The many newly-married included women from Greece, Egypt and Poland and other Europeans and their servicemen husbands. We were allocated cabins, and I was to share one with two other servicemen's wives. Our husbands were separate and had to sleep in hammocks. I saw Bill only on deck during the day; we couldn't even have our meals together. Servicemen were down below deck and were only allowed to see their wives during the day on the decks.

The journey was terrible, it lasted ten days, and throughout all that time I was seasick and couldn't eat anything. Every time I walked into the dining room and saw the waves through the portholes I immediately had to

The Durban Castle

go back to my cabin, as I just couldn't face any food. Bill fed me on dry cream crackers when we met on deck. It was a horrible voyage, very miserable, nothing but the high seas all around us. I wished I'd never come, and there was no way of getting off. It seemed a very stormy crossing to me, although Bill thought it was calm! Perhaps if we had been together it would have been easier to bear.

Six years after that day in February 1940 when my life had changed forever, I was on my own, without my parents this time, going into the unknown yet again. I was travelling to yet another country not knowing what to expect. Meeting Bill's parents, wondering what would they be like, was very difficult to deal with on my own. I was still only 22 and desperately missing my family.

On the tenth day of the voyage I felt the ship stopping and I looked through the porthole to see land, green grass and trees. You can't imagine my joy to know that I would be able to put my feet on firm ground again. I think I had breakfast that morning, but I don't really remember, I was too happy to be on land again.

We left the ship that morning, November 9th 1946, and Bill was with me when we disembarked at Southampton. After we had collected our luggage we went to a little café and for the first time in my life (but not the last) I had English fish and chips, which were delicious after all that time at sea. It was my first big meal, not having had much to eat on board the ship. It was so tasty.

We now had to take the train to Blackpool in the North of England, via London. We travelled almost all night – five hours – arriving at Blackpool North Station at 5 am in the dark, in a very thick cold fog. I had never seen anything like it. It was so depressing, unwelcoming, grey and damp that I thought to myself I would have gone back if I could. What a contrast to the beautiful countries I had just left.

We took a taxi to Bill's parents' house, and arrived at the house still in the dark. A tall, white-haired woman, his mother Alice, opened the door and I thought, 'she looks nice, I think I'll be happy here'. She embraced Bill, the son she hadn't seen for five years, and I was just standing there in the hall waiting whilst they hugged before Bill introduced me. Alice just said hello and that was all; I didn't really feel welcome. There was no embrace, no friendliness, no warmth on her part. I was away from my own parents, missing love and warmth in a strange country, just a young woman really, but there was very little welcome for me and I'd had such hopes.

This was a sign of things to come. It was many months later that things started to go horribly wrong. My mother-in-law was constantly hostile towards me and I had had enough. I couldn't cope with such an inhospitable woman. I had already gone through so much hardship that I could not take any more and I thought she might have understood and been more thoughtful. I told Bill I was going to stay with my sister in London until he found somewhere else for us to live. I'd put up with this for too long, and I was worn out by it. At this stage I had two babies to look after which thankfully gave me something to focus on.

Jasia came from London as soon as she could to collect me. Bill loaded everything, cases and children and me onto a train (he was now working for British Rail). He was distraught that we were leaving, but I said to him that he would have more time and incentive to look for something for us and he really didn't have a choice, I wasn't coming back. Of course my in-laws apologised to Bill, in fact they fell over themselves with apologies, but not to me, and I knew that things would not be any different. They had made it very clear they didn't want me there.

I stayed with my sister for a few weeks, and it wasn't long before Bill found a house for us. I came back from London with the children and we moved into our new home - we couldn't have been happier. It was heaven being on our own with our two babies. We didn't have much furniture but we were happy. There was a cooker, so I could cook some nice meals, we had somewhere to sleep, there was a garden, I had a very loving husband and knew that together we would get on with life.

I never knew why my mother-in-law was so cruel. In later years I welcomed her into my home so that she would get to know her grandchildren. We never spoke of it. She behaved as though nothing had happened and never apologised.

All was not milk and honey in this new land. There were difficulties, and it was hard to adapt to a very different life, mixing with people when shopping for essentials, for example, and trying to converse in English, which I still wasn't very good at. People weren't openly hostile towards me nor were they over welcoming, they were just accepting. They too had to adjust to a different life after a devastating war and with people of many nationalities now living amongst them. It was a learning experience for us all.

Many refugees would find it difficult after arriving in England. Alone, still in a state of shock and perhaps bereft of hope, they would search crowds for any sign of family they'd lost in their exodus from Russia, scrutinising faces in church, shops, on the bus and the street for any recognition of family or friends, hoping to be reunited with just one familiar face. They would search for many years.

Alicja and Bill, 1951

THE FAMILY REUNITED

My parents and Janusz came to England in 1948, followed by the other family members, Walery and Ziuta and family soon after. As Adam and Walery and their families had been considered 'class enemies' it was an easy decision to make to come to England. From 1945 up to 1953 Polish underground leaders were sentenced to death and executed for 'sabotage', and some 20,000 were murdered. Former deportees and other 'undesirables' were also treated most harshly. England would be a safe haven. There was no future in Poland unless you were a communist.

They arrived in Liverpool after a very long journey from Port Said in February 1948. We had waited for the ship for hours, looking out for them. The seas were very rough, too severe for the boat to dock for a day or two, so we had to come back, which was very frustrating. We did spy my parents and Janusz waving his scarf like mad and the excitement I felt I will never forget. We were so close to reunion.

When they were eventually able to disembark they had

to go through the process of formal registration. They were interviewed and issued with Certificate of Registration (Aliens Order 1920) documents and recorded as ENA 9012203, ENA9012204 and ENA9012205, which took some time.

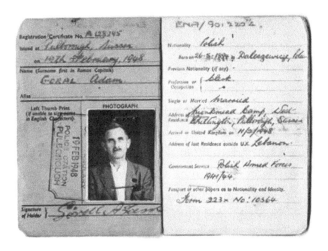

Certificate of Registration for Adam Goral (Aliens Order 1920) No: 128295 – 19th February 1948 Exempt from registration 29th May 1961

We waited in a reception area for such a long time. There were many hundreds of refugees to be processed, so we tried to be patient, Finally they appeared, and I cannot describe our emotions. It was so very intense that we could barely talk. We held each other so very tightly. Oh how I had missed my family, my mother especially. It was so good to see them.

Our reunion, however, was very short lived. Adam, Kazia and Janusz had been allocated places at a camp in Five Oaks, near Brighton, and had to travel there by train. They stayed there for a few days and were then placed in Pulborough, registered with the West Sussex Constabulary, and issued with clothing and food coupons. They were to stay there for several months and were then moved to other camps, usually unused army barracks, in Horsham, Ely, which was surrounded by beautiful forests and reminded us of the Osada, and then onto Helstern in Lincs.

We were able to visit them and they were able to come to us. Their registration cards record visits to us in Lytham St Anne's, from those camps up to December 1950 and then visits to us from Victoria and Brixton in London up to 1958. Each visit to and from was stamped by the Metropolitan Police or Lancashire Constabulary. They were finally exempt from registering their movements in 1961.

My parents came to live with us in 1950 when they were able to leave the camps. We started decorating the house, putting lino on the floor and varnishing the floorboards. With rugs on the floors it was looking much nicer. We were so excited and were ready to welcome them.

Kazia, Tony, Teri, Ala and Adam, Lytham St Annes 1951

Ala, Janusz and Jasia

My parents stayed with us for about four years, but they found it quite lonely, as they didn't speak English and consequently found it very difficult to mix. They needed to be in a Polish community, and it wasn't long before they left us to go to London, where there was a big Polish community slowly building. Most displaced people coming to England after the war had headed to the capital, and small Polish and Jewish communities were springing up. St Anne's was only a small town and there wasn't a Polish community for them to become involved with. They were still young enough to be more active and needed something constructive to do. Teri and Tony were at convent by then and although Adam and Kazia enjoyed taking them to and from school and teaching them Polish, it wasn't keeping them busy enough. Adam had his garden and Kazia busied herself in the home whilst Bill and I were at work but it wasn't really enough, they needed people of their own age. We understood and with sad hearts saw them off to London.

Kazia and Adam

They lived with Jasia and Bolcio in Vauxhall and then later in Brixton, helping to raise Alec whilst Jasia and Bolcio worked. Janusz also shared the house in Brixton which they had bought with a friend. Putting down roots in a new country was expensive, so sharing costs, especially the purchase of a house, was quite common. They later moved to Forest Hill, sharing the lower part of a large house with Janusz, who had by then married Pamela and had two young daughters, Anita and Krysia.

Adam was a very devout believer in his faith and dedicated all of his life to charity, helping to raise money for the poor and starving in Africa. He was also very active for the local Polish community and helped to raise funds

Kazia and Adam in London

for the purchase of their own church in Balham which to this day is a thriving parish and society and a meeting place for the Osadnikow Kresowych. This society is made up of the surviving relatives of the families of the eastern borderlands, survivors of Stalins ethnic cleansing programme as he was. The president of this society is Ryszard Grzybowski, a friend of Jasia's, a leading member of this society; we met him at her funeral in December 2011.

When Bolcio died they moved back to Streatham to support Jasia and Alec always on hand for whoever needed their help. In their later years they moved to a Polish home in Corby and later to Antokol in Sidcup.

Jasia had been in England before the rest of us, in September 1946, and she lived and worked in Everleigh, Wiltshire, as a teacher in the Polish refugees' camp. She then moved to Guildford after finishing her further education course. She had met her future husband Bolcio (Boleslaw) in Guildford. He was a university graduate and physical training instructor who had taken part in the 1936 Olympics in Berlin, a footballer in Poland and a veteran of the Battle of Monte Cassino. They married on 23rd July 1949 and settled in Victoria, and their son Alec was born in 1950.

In 1954 they moved to Brixton and later on to Streatham in 1962. In 1963, without any indication of ill health, Bolcio died of a coronary at the age of only 49. Jasia remarried in 1966, to Bruno Misik, an artist, who spent a lot of time in his retirement renovating the Stations of the Cross at Balham Polish church. He died in 1990.

Jasia then devoted more of herself to the Polish

Jasia and Bolcio

Jasia

community. She was a most colourful personality, some acquaintances likening her to Zsa Zsa Gabor, having a very strong Polish accent and always being so beautifully dressed. She became a stalwart figure in the Balham Polish community, running social clubs for the elderly and lonely and a charity for Polish orphans in Warsaw (Pruszkow) for which she collected copious amounts of money by advertising in the Polish Press. She moved to Balham in 2000, where she cared for her then partner Stanislaw Raymond, another veteran of Monte Cassino who had suffered serious head wounds and in later years dementia.

This all took a huge toll on Jasia's health, and after his death in 2009 her own health deteriorated dramatically and she battled hard over the next two years. In December 2010 she was diagnosed with secondary lung cancer and struggled to come to terms with it and the considerable pain it caused her. I visited and stayed with her several times during this period throughout 2010/11 and was there in November 2011 when she died whilst a carer was tending to her needs.

Janusz

I knew it was inevitable but it was still an awful shock, as my little sister was such a vibrant person. Teri took it badly, as they had been very close, Jasia also being her godmother. We had cared and fought for each other throughout our travels to and from Russia, and Kazia and Adam, Walery and Ziuta, Janusz, Marysia and now Jasia, were all gone. I was now the only one of the family left who had survived the wartime hell created by Stalin. I suddenly felt quite alone.

Janusz had gone to Glasgow to continue his education before moving in with Jasia and Bolcio in Victoria around 1951. He studied restorative dentistry, but gave this up to move into the hospitality trade and work in the hotels of London, the Berkeley, the Bedford and then the Savoy where he worked until retirement at 65. He met many famous faces here, the most memorable being the Queen Mother.

Janusz with HM The Queen Mother at the Savoy

Marysia had come to England in 1946 with Jasia and then had settled in West London with her parents Walery and Ziuta and her brother Wlodek. She married Wiesiek in 1950 and later with their three children, Marek, Ania and

Back row: Wiesiek, Marysia, Wlodek, Walery. Front row: Genia, Marek, Kazia, c. 1957

Marysia in London, c. 1965

Ewa, they moved to Brockley. Marek has lived and worked in Warsaw for many years and has three children, Adam, Marcin and Izabella. He recently became grandfather to a baby girl, Janina. Ania and Ewa live and work in Kent.

It wasn't until some time after their arrival in England that Uncle Walery and Aunty Ziuta had devastating news about their younger son Zbyszek, who had joined the Polish underground in western Poland at the outbreak of war. He had been shot by his drunken 'best friend' on returning to barracks from leave, after seeing Aunty Genia in Lublin. His friend had demanded to see Zbyszek's pass on entry to the camp and Zbyszek's reply was "but you know me, I've just shown you my pass", but his friend fired at point-blank range and killed him. He was only 23. He had survived the war only to be shot by his best friend! The exact details are unclear, and why his friend was drunk and on duty will never be known, but the family were shattered. I don't know what action if any was taken by Uncle and Aunty, or what happened to the young man who fired the gun.

THOSE WHO STAYED BEHIND

My Aunt Genia and her daughter Halina survived the war with her husband Wladislaw in western Poland. Halina married Wiesek Morawiec, and both worked as doctors in Stalowa Wola. Bruno died at quite an early age but Halina still lives in Stalowa Wola and in her 80s now continues her work as a specialist in rheumatology. They had a son, Macius, who practises law in Warsaw.

Genia, c 1976

Sisters reunited - Kazia and Genia

After Genia died, Halina found a letter whilst sorting out her belongings, from Sofia, Aunty Genia's mother and my grandmother. The details are quite vague but it describes Sofia's experiences and survival during the Russian occupation and later behind the Iron Curtain. We do not have access to this information so we don't know what happened to Sofia or how she had managed to survive on her own during such harsh times, as she had been quite elderly. Genia had related some of these details to us in the phone calls we shared over the years, but the details are vague as she had to be so careful. Conversations had to be short and they were not able to discuss personal details.

The whole population was trapped under a dictatorship which claimed to represent all the people, but in fact represented only the worker and peasant classes, which were more easily controlled. All others were 'the enemy'. Every single aspect of life was controlled under the Kremlin's direction, assisted by the police, militia and the party bureauracrats. Control was by fear, hunger and lies.

The communist way of operating was in three steps: plan an effective deceit, execute a ruthless crime and then justify it with an outrageous lie.

Our Polish relatives were brought up in a dark and

inaccessible place, where they had to observe the harsh party line. It would be easy to assume that to successfully work as doctors as both Halina and Wiesiek, did so as not to be considered enemies of the state but a necessity, they toed the party line more readily. It certainly allowed them more freedom, as well as an apartment with two bedrooms! They were able, with Aunty Genia, to visit us in England and allowed to educate their son to a good standard, which the ordinary Pole found very difficult to access. Education and advancement were denied you, especially if you were a former deportee, or another designated 'enemy of the state' or a relative of one.

We have no knowledge whatsoever of their political affiliations, or how they had lived through communism, such is the lack of information. Were they relieved at Poland's eventual freedom from the curse of communism? Or were they hard-line party activists who, having lost their party status, suddenly became on a more equal footing with the rest of the democratic population?

We do know that life was generally very difficult. People queued even for toilet rolls and to obtain the most basic of needs. There were empty shelves in the shops, intermittently supplied by the mostly unproductive collective farms. Shops were owned by the state and run by their favoured ones, who stole most of the food for themselves. The only shops overflowing with goods were the propaganda 'shops', peddling the state pronouncements! We were all sending food parcels and clothing parcels to Aunty Genia up to the 1980s. People did help each other to survive, you had to, if it was only keeping someone's place in one of the many queues!

We know that people where possible paid for items in

cash so that transactions could not be traced by the state. We know people only had short conversations for fear that too much interaction would put them in danger of being arrested and interrogated. There were over 100,000 state informants, which is why people were so guarded and so isolated. You say too much and the information could be manipulated and used against you, so to avoid arrest and interrogation you become an informant! Criticize the state-controlled news programme openly and you were in big trouble. You were a rebel if you listened to Radio Free Europe or if you had access to American television stations you were in very serious trouble. If you were found out, you would be on your way to the gulag! It all sounds ridiculous, but this was the ghastly and miserable existence through communism. We can only assume that this is perhaps why they were so reluctant to divulge any information. We have freedom of thought and word and take it so much for granted we can't imagine a life without it.

We do know that Wiesiek strongly disapproved of our Catholic faith. Janusz, on one of his visits to Poland, once tackled him about this and asked if he was a communist, but of course Wiesiek brushed this aside. He did not however join the family in church for very long before leaving on an 'urgent' matter! He was very critical of the family for not returning to Poland, and made his views known to us. There may have been resentment about this as he was by marriage related to deportees and this would have been known to the Soviet authorities.

Many Poles who had not returned to their homeland after the war were vilified, and this put those family members who had returned at a great disadvantage. They were blacklisted and suffered even more deprivation and hostility.

Even after communism it may be extremely difficult to let go of old habits and adapt to democracy and free speech, chat freely in the street, criticize the news without looking over your shoulder.

We have regrettably lost touch with our Polish relatives, Halina and Macius (Radomski link). Jasia and I were in touch with Halina by phone on an occasional basis and Alec tracked Macius down via Google, and both he and Teri had initial contact via email with him. Despite many other attempts by both Alec and Teri to develop a relationship we are still not able to learn what exactly happened to Sofia. There were some reports that she was shot by the NKVD in eastern Poland, but we have no way of investigating this to confirm it.

The bond between the Radomskis, Kazia and brother Walery and their families was very strong; it had to be to survive such massive upheaval and deprivation. They almost died from starvation and from illnesses they became susceptible to, malaria, typhus, dysentery and typhoid. They weren't heroic, but luck and insignificant circumstances did play a part in their survival.

They supported each other in freedom and assimilated themselves to a new country without any great difficulty, working and living happily and productively until retirement and beyond.

Kazia and Adam, Walery and Ziuta are long gone; they died without being able to revisit their old country, which was a great regret to them. Wlodek also died before his time.

Janusz, Marysia and Jasia were lost to us more recently. Each and every one remains forever in our memories, and we raise a 'Polish measure' to them at certain times of the year. Their bond was broken not by Stalin but simply by the passing of time. Z Bogiem.`

Great Grandfather Wladyslaw Bielawski

Grandparents – Wladyslaw & Sophia Radomski

Family Radomski, formerly
Bielawski – The blood line

ND - #0032 - 270225 - C180 - 203/127/10 - PB - 9781909544765 - Matt Lamination